"My life was a high-speed chase. *What's the Rush?* has taught me to slow down and enjoy the journey! Thanks, Jim!"

—*Frank Pacetta, author of* Don't Fire Them, Fire Them Up!

"With good advice and insights, Ballard proves that fitness, good health, and contentment are indeed 'all in your head.' "

—*Pete Egoscue, author of* Pain Free: A Revolutionary Method for Stopping Chronic Pain

"Peace, tranquillity, balance, and, best of all, feeling in control while still leading a fast-paced, productive life. This is no 'sit at the side of the stream and watch life float by' book. *What's the Rush?* teaches how to ride the white-water rapids of life as a full participant and enjoy the ride! Jim Ballard has written a delightful, charming, challenging, and effective guide to achieving balance in life and for this I am in his debt."

—*Sheldon Bowles, coauthor of the bestselling books* Raving Fans *and* Gung Ho!

"Jim Ballard has written a self-help book . . . about running. Really. Running. And it's built on several other seeming absurdities. Take it easier and run faster. Get into a dream state and you will deal better with reality. Stop trying so hard and success will come. Walk and run at the same time. Let the race run you instead of you running. Ballard shows that these paradoxes apply to all of life and supports that idea with plenty of examples, interesting exercises, and pithy quotes. As someone who believes that in life paradox is the rule and not the exception, I think he may be on to something."

—*Richard Farson, author of* Management of the Absurd

What's the Rush?

Broadway Books · New York

What's the Rush?

a dreamrunner's guide

Step Out of the Race,

Free Your Mind,

Change Your Life

JAMES BALLARD

BROADWAY

WHAT'S THE RUSH? Copyright © 1999 by James Ballard. All rights reserved. Printed in the United States of America. No part of this book may be reproduced or transmitted in any form or by any means, electronic or mechanical, including photocopying, recording, or by any information storage and retrieval system, without written permission from the publisher. For information, address Broadway Books, a division of Random House, Inc., 1540 Broadway, New York, NY 10036.

Broadway Books titles may be purchased for business or promotional use or for special sales. For information, please write to: Special Markets Department, Random House, Inc., 1540 Broadway, New York, NY 10036.

BROADWAY BOOKS and its logo, a letter B bisected on the diagonal, are trademarks of Broadway Books, a division of Random House, Inc.

Library of Congress Cataloging-in-Publication Data
Ballard, Jim, 1933–
    What's the rush? : step out of the race, free your mind, change your life / by James Ballard. — 1st ed.
    p.   m.
    ISBN 0-7679-0310-2
    1. Self-actualization (Psychology)   I. Title.
BF637.S4B34   1999
158.1—DC21   98-28980
                                                                  CIP

FIRST EDITION

Designed by Pei Loi Koay
Line drawings by Jackie Aher
Photo illustrations by Amherst Camera

99   00   01   02   03   10   9   8   7   6   5   4   3   2   1

Contents

We are no other than a moving row

Of Magic Shadow-shapes that come and go

Round with the Sun-illumin'd Lantern held

In Midnight by the Master of the Show.

. . . .

Omar Khayyám

Foreword

When Jim Ballard asked me if I would write the foreword to his book *What's the Rush?* I was thrilled that the book would be available to people to read and re-read as many times as needed. I say "re-read" because when I concluded my first reading of the pre-publication manuscript I was sorry to see it end; I felt as if I'd lost a good friend. But then I realized my friend was always there for me, and now I find myself reading parts of *What's the Rush?* almost daily. Reading this book sets me up for what Stephen Covey, author of *The Seven Habits of Highly Effective People,* says we need every day: a personal victory. And the earlier in the day that occurs for me, the better.

I am excited that *What's the Rush?* is available now to help us all create our own personal victories. Now many other readers will get to know my friend Jim Ballard through his two wonderful gifts—writing and personal coaching. Jim has been my behind-the-scenes co-author for many of my bestselling books, including *The Power of Ethical Management* with Norman Vincent Peale, *Everyone's A Coach* with legendary football coach Don Shula, *Mission Possible* with Terry Waghorn, and *Managing By Values* with Michael O'Connor. Because I know Jim's talent and depth as a writer, I know you are in for a treat.

Ever since I met Jim 25 years ago in Amherst, Massachusetts, he has been an important person in my life. Whenever I've been faced with a major decision or choice, Jim has been there as my personal coach to help me see things more clearly. Jim never gives me the answers; he listens to me, and in some magical way the right road always appears. For example, after the phenomenal success of *The One Minute Manager*© it seemed to me I had two choices. I could get a distorted image of my own importance, let my ego eat my brain, and start to think I was a big deal—or, I could choose wonderment and attempt to look at life and success with a different set of glasses. Jim Ballard helped me make that second choice. That was when I learned a very important truth from Jim: the truth about our two selves.

Each of us has an outer or task-oriented self, and an inner or spiritual self. While the outer or everyday self concentrates on achieving and accomplishing, the inner self focuses on who we really are, where we're really going, and what our relationship is to the spiritual energy around us. Jim says it's important to take time to consciously "enter" each day because the inner self takes longer to wake up in the morning. Most people jump out of bed each day and are into their day before the inner self has been awakened. In my discussions with Jim I've come to learn that unless I wake up my inner self in the morning I can get "off purpose" during the day.

Part of awakening my spiritual self every morning is recognizing that God is the source of all good. In my morning runs/walks the *What's the Rush?* concept that has helped me the most is what Jim calls "Being Run." Imagine yourself standing still and the street moving under you. You are Being Run. What a wonderful way to realize that you are not the doer in life but the instrument of action of a larger plan. This process has made me realize that in a very real sense Spencer Johnson and I didn't write *The One Minute Manager*©, it wrote us.

The day after I read the pre-publication manuscript of *What's the Rush?* I was scheduled to give a talk to a group of top managers. What a talk that turned out to be! I'd given that same address at least five times before, but never like this. Everything flowed without any effort. Reading *What's the Rush?* had put me in the "Being Run" mindset, so that instead of talking I could "be talked." The whole experience, for me and for the audience, was transformed. When I got myself out of the way, truths could be shared which were deeper, simpler, and more important than I could have come up with myself.

In my travels around the world I have found many people who are grappling with their inner selves and seeking spiritual connectedness. People are working harder, running faster; they may even be reaping many material benefits. But their hunger for meaning isn't satisfied. It's as if they're saying, "After all this effort, is this all there is?" I'm convinced that this book is coming at just the right time to help large numbers of people answer this question. This is a book you can use to train yourself to get balance back in your life. I'm excited at the prospect of Jim Ballard's becoming your personal coach, just as he is mine. Open your heart and mind to his ideas. As you do, you'll discover an inner self, a source of peace and fulfillment that will help you go beyond any success you ever imagined.

—*Ken Blanchard*

Introduction

> I wipe a mirror and place it in
>
> your hands.
>
> *Edward Carpenter*

What's the rush? Good question for most of us in these turbulent times. With all the stresses and demands on us, it seems we must run faster and faster just to keep up. But where is all this rushing getting us? Is it satisfying for us? Are we doing more tasks, but finding less meaning in them? If so, it's time to take stock. We must separate what is important from what is merely urgent. Are you happy with the pace and tenor of your daily life? Do you like the way things are going? If not, this book will help you to make changes. It will guide you to *step out of the race . . . free your mind . . . change your life.*

Living in today's turbulent world, it's easy to feel fearful about the uncertainties that accompany rapid change. Lacking assurance about how things will turn out, it seems easier to just run faster, do the next thing, fit one more thing in, and tolerate the frustration and exhaustion, than to stop, take a look at what's going on, and begin to take action to correct the situation.

Many people today see themselves as victims of a world in constant change. Uncertainty haunts them. They wake up each morning with a vague sense of dread, a low-grade anxiety associated with their inability to predict or control their futures. They feel powerless; they worry about the future, about money, about their health. It seems they can do nothing to change things. But they can do something—they can **change their minds.**

Experience is not what happens to us; it is what we *do* with what happens to us. This means we don't need to change the world, but the way we look at it. What is required is a self-science: the scientist is the individual self; the laboratory is the mind; the experimental activity is *dreamrunning,* the subject of this book. What is *dreamrunning?* It is the practice of deliberately shifting attention away from the mind's accustomed ways of defining experience into another perspective, where the self appears to be not the cause but the instrument of action. When a person has this experience, he or she achieves a balance between "making things happen" and "letting things happen" that feels right.

This balance removes stress and makes life more enjoyable and fascinating. Worry goes away, alarm and tragedy disappear. It seems whatever happens is meant to happen, because while we occupy this space of the mind we are free of the fears that restrict us in our ability to deal effectively and creatively with life. We experience a natural connectedness with things. We can see clearly so that we recognize solutions which formerly were hidden from us.

The core experience in *What's the Rush?* is captured in the words of South African jazz pianist Abdullah Ibrahim: "I am not a player, I am played." It is the exhilarating realization that we are not the "doers" of the activity in which we engage. This experience tunes us in to the life force that is behind all our activities, the source of energy by whose agency we are enabled to think and act. By practicing *dreamrunning* techniques we align ourselves with the hidden wellspring of our being, which goes unknown and unacknowledged when human beings mistakenly believe that they are the originators of their actions.

What's the Rush? is designed to help people use their minds to catch up with their experience. Why running? Because in these turbulent times we are all running—running to keep up, to stay ahead, to get everything done. Running is a metaphor for all the hurrying and rushing about that people are doing these days. *What's the Rush?* is not so much about jogging the body as jogging the mind out of its ruts. The goal is to achieve and to maintain a state of "inner fitness." This inner fitness, achieved by self-effort and practice, creates an antidote for the growing sense of dislocation, the spiritual emptiness so many are feeling today. The conviction that drives this book is that our true home, our rightful sense of belonging and security, is found not in the outer world, but within ourselves.

THE THREE NOETIC PRACTICES

What's the Rush? is a manual for how to use the mind to be happy by gaining inner control amidst the uncertainties of life. Things we used to count on and take for granted are shifting before our eyes: job security, permanence of home and career, neighborhood continuity, dependability of institutions such as marriage and family, our role as a nation, etc. In the world of business, all is in flux—markets, customer needs, and competitors seem to change overnight. Even though we don't have much control over events and circumstances, we can train ourselves to be assured of an internal control that brings us peace and well-being. This book describes why we have lost this important sense of inner control. It shows how to recognize the signals that tell us we have lost it. And it suggests ways to regain it. I call these techniques for gaining control Noetic Practices.

The word *noetic* (from the Greek *nous,* meaning mind or ways of knowing) refers to the scientific exploration of mind and consciousness as the roots of human experience. The noetic self-science described in this book is about transforming our experience by deliberately and continuously changing the way we see things. Working within the laboratory of our own experience, we develop our ability to see things in new ways, and in the process we come to know ourselves.

This practice is based on what might be termed *militant optimism*—a ferocious commitment to being happy. As students of this discipline, we begin by abandoning our lifelong careers of trying to change the world. Whenever we find that we are stressed or upset, rather than assigning cause or blame to the outside event, we assume distortion in the way we are perceiving things. This is more than "attitude adjustment." It is the practice of truth—making our perceptions match the way things actually are. We are taking each unhappiness-making instance as a personal challenge, an opportunity to go inside and examine our belief structures. By this process we gradually gain mastery over reality (defined as "the way I am seeing things").

By no means does this commitment to scrutinizing our own mental processes imply abandonment of ambition, or of thinking for ourselves, or of asserting our way in the world. This optimistic self-science is based on a ruthless examination of distorted notions and attitudes and on a deep trust in intuitive perception. When successful, we achieve an elegant balance between the rigidity of intellect and the fluidity of intuition. Maintaining this balance sharpens thinking to a fine creative edge, awakening and attuning wise discrimination. Noetic Practices involve us in a sort of psychic alchemy which has the magical power to transform our experience. Paradoxically, the very simplicity of the practices makes them easily accessible for use in extremely complex and demanding circumstances.

I examine three Noetic Practices. They are:

1. Dreaming the World
2. Reframing Experience
3. Playing with Time

As we regularly and consciously activate each of these Noetic Practices, we become more attuned with life as it unfolds moment by moment. We begin to develop an ability to deal more effectively with our daily experience. Instead of being tumbled about and disoriented in the chaotic rapids of our circumstances, we can view the stream of change from a calm perspective.

ASCENDING THE NOETIC PRACTICES (NP) PYRAMID

. . . .

When people grapple with the uncertainties of relentless change, they can easily come to feel like helpless victims of all the changes. Getting beyond this victim state of mind means essentially rising above it. The three Practices outlined above enable us to do this, provided they are activated continuously and deliberately as a mind-management program. A symbol that combines elevation by means of three forces is the three-sided pyramid; it is used here to illustrate how use of the Noetic Practices elevates us above the churning waters of change, giving us a loftier perspective and allowing intuition* to kick in and reveal the truth about our situation.

* The great teacher Paramahansa Yogananda (1893–1952) defined intuition as "that directly perceiving faculty of the soul that at once knows the truth about anything, requiring no medium of sense experience or reason. It does not consist in believing a thing, but in knowing it directly and unmistakably. It does not contradict. It is always supported by a right sense of perception, reason, and inference, although it does not depend upon any data whatsoever offered by the senses or the mind. A real intuition can never be wrong. Everyone possesses this quality more or less. Like any other faculty, it must be cultivated."

The following diagrams and descriptions provide an overview of the general developmental steps described so far. By depicting the changing trends of the past few decades, these pictorials sum up the main themes and highlight the need for the practices this book presents.

STEP 1.

Understand the nature and impact of current change.

We have entered a stream of continuous change, unparalleled for its complexity. Never having lived with this amount of unpredictability and uncertainty before, we are confused and disoriented by it.

Stream of Change

Admit that what we are currently doing is not working.

Living in an environment of great turbulence, we typically re-act by speeding up, rushing about, trying to keep up with all the changes. When we operate in a state of constant stress and anxiety, our view of life becomes distorted and we develop tunnel vision. The physical attributes of the material world—time and space—assume monstrous proportions that restrict our thinking and limit our ability to create. Seen from this di-minished perspective, the material world appears to be all there is, and time appears to be a limited resource. When people use expressions like "too many balls in the air," or "too much on my plate," they are seeing things from a perspective of time-scarcity. Frequently, they are overwhelmed by all the changes coming at them and feel victimized.

People mistakenly think they must maintain control—as if life and success were all about overcoming and conquering. They speak of "managing" change. (Given the amount of change people must deal with at the close of this century, this makes about as much sense as "managing" the weather.) This false assumption, coupled with the hopeless activity of trying to control what happens to them, creates an extremely limited state of consciousness which I call *littlethink. Littlethink* is being at the mercy of circumstances and conditions of material life, with no apparent choice but to cope and react to them. *Littlethink* is the opposite of being calm and happy, confident and contented no matter what may happen. It is the worrisome state of mind that can never be at peace, never simply let go of concerns, relax, and *be!* A mind in the *littlethink* condition is reduced to thinking small, dealing in particles. It is caged in its own limitations.

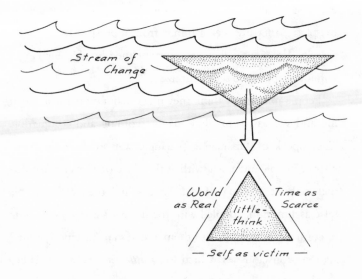

Learn skills to leverage our experience of change.

The Noetic Practices (NPs) presented in this book help us change the way we think. Noetic Practice 1, Dreaming the World, helps us redefine the nature of our world and what we perceive as reality. Noetic Practice 2, Reframing Experience, enables us to stop perceiving and acting like victims. Noetic Practice 3, Playing with Time, allows us to come at life from a reality of time-abundance instead of scarcity. When we ascend the NP pyramid, we transform our experience of everyday change so that it becomes enjoyable and rewarding.

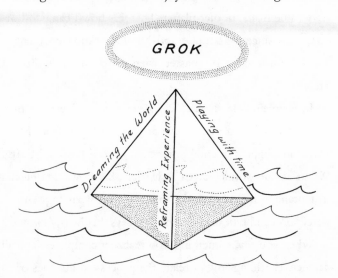

STEP 4.

Using the new, empowered perspective, choose right action in the moment.

When, through combined use of the three NPs, our perspective is of sufficient breadth, we begin to *grok*. What is *grokking?* Imagine for a moment having developed such proficiency in using the Noetic Practices that you are able to move through each day in the bliss known only to one who is the consummate master of self and experience. As I cast about for a way to describe this state of enlarged awareness—the ability to see all things, as it were, from the apex of the NP pyramid—I have imagined that a person possessing this power would almost have to be from another planet. That was how I came to borrow, with sincere gratitude and humble acknowledgment, a word from a story by master science fiction writer Robert Heinlein.

In Heinlein's classic tale, *Stranger in a Strange Land,* the protagonist is a young man newly arrived on Earth from Mars, where inhabitants' mental powers far exceed those of Earth. When, to the wonder of earthdwellers, he shows that he can instantaneously understand a thing, utterly bypassing sensory perception and rational inference, he says that he *groks it.*

When you *grok* something, you realize it completely and all at once. Earthlings might relate the process to hunches or to

ESP. My objective is to remove the awe from the skill by stating that *grokking* is something that each of us can already do. Simply put, *grokking* is inner knowing, or complete reliance on intuition. Our capacity to intuit—to know something without knowing how we know it—is what Einstein was speaking of when he said, "There comes a time when the mind takes a higher plane of knowledge but can never prove how it got there. All great discoveries have involved such a leap."

Another way I describe this state of exalted awareness is through a story I tell in my training seminars.

The owner of a factory purchased an electronic master-machine designed to run all the other machinery in the plant. One day this machine quit, and the whole factory went down. The owner and his managers spent time fussing over the machine, studying the manual, pushing buttons, kicking it, etc., all to no avail. Frantic, the factory owner called the place where he had bought the machine.

"Lucky for you," he was told, "the inventor of that machine is in town. He'll be right over."

Soon a limousine drew up at the factory door, and a little man in a blue suit, dark beard and dark glasses got out. He was carrying a small satchel. "Where is it?" he demanded. The owner, his employees in tow, escorted the little man to the mysterious machine. Giving the control console a cursory glance, the inventor went around to the rear of the machine where no one had thought of looking. He began feeling around on a certain panel until he located a certain spot. He then reached into his case and took out a small rubber hammer. Poising the hammer above the spot as people held their breath, he tapped lightly, just once, on that precise spot. As if by magic, the great machine started up; the factory was running again!

All the people went back to work. As the owner walked the inventor out to his car he was profuse in his praise.

"This was wonderful! One tap with a hammer—I never saw anything like it! You don't know the expense you've saved me. Just send me the bill!"

"I can give you the bill right now," said the man.

"Fine," said the owner.

The inventor sat down and wrote out a bill. When the owner read the bill, he saw that it was for $10,000.00.

"There must be some mistake here," he protested. Ten thousand dollars? Why, all you did was tap once with a hammer. I want this bill itemized."

The little man quickly wrote out a second bill, gave it to the factory owner, and left. The owner looked at the bill. It read:

For tapping once with a hammer	$ 1.00
For knowing where to tap	9,999.00

This story's conclusion is usually greeted by laughter, proof that the intuitive minds of listeners have resonated with its message of leveraging.

Dreamrunner advisory

. . . .

Much effort, wrongly placed, is a waste. Little effort, rightly placed, is worth much.

When we have taught ourselves to rise above the randomness and uncertainty associated with *littlethink,* we become focused, direct and purposeful in our actions. We *grok* the situation and act appropriately because we "know where to tap."

Grokking, or acting from a purely intuitive source, not only leads to deep happiness—bliss—it also enables us to bring personal order out of environmental chaos. Free to reason and act from an inner source, rather than forced to react to outer stimuli, we learn to live comfortably with impermanence. Our satisfaction is deep and lasting, for it comes from inside us rather than from outside. We become inhabitants of an entirely new dimension of experience from which our view is loftier and more far-reaching.

There is an apparent contradiction here. On the one hand I am saying that most people are trapped in *littlethink,* the victim state. On the other hand I am saying that it is our need for control that is keeping us unempowered. How can these be harmonized? Only by realization of a paradox:

Dreamrunner advisory
. . . .

By giving up control, we gain power.

In a world where things seem to be flying faster and faster, even sometimes threatening to fly apart, it can bring great peace, even for a brief moment, to relinquish our supposed control of every-thing. *We are not in control anyway; it is acting as if we are that exhausts us.* There is a way to use this realization to empower ourselves. The process of that empowerment is what this book is about.

OVERVIEW OF THE BOOK
. . . .

What's the Rush? consists of two main parts: theory (the ideas behind the practices) and practices (the collection of *dreamrunning* techniques called Recipes for the Sole). The Recipes have been interspersed among and between the chapters in order to remind the reader that the self-science I call *dreamrunning* is not merely a collection of concepts, it is about things you actually do with your mind and body.

Chapter One, "On the Run," explores the problem for which *dreamrunning* is the treatment. It shows how change itself has changed over the past few decades, culminating in the present condition of "constant white water." Amidst this turmoil, we are in danger of drowning—unable to keep up with our new ways of living—because of our old ways of thinking.

Chapter Two, "Escape from Littlethink," is the outcomes-and-benefits chapter. It details what *dreamrunning* can do for you. This chapter hints at the joyous power to be found in using the three NP's to integrate life around a purpose greater than ourselves.

Each of the next three chapters explores one of the Noetic Practices separately. Chapter Three, "Dreaming the World," is a personal account of how I came upon *dreamrunning*. It develops the idea that the world we see is really a dream, and that there are decided advantages to seeing it this way. This chapter presents Noetic Practice 1.

The second Noetic Practice is the focus of Chapter Four, "Reframing Experience." This chapter examines the process of perception and explains how, through the activity of *dreamrunning,* we can practice shifting the way we experience the world.

"Playing with Time" is the title of Chapter Five. It is our sense of time that most troubles us in this closing decade of a speeded-up century. This chapter demonstrates Noetic Practice 3; how we can achieve great power by concentrating attention in the present moment.

The concluding chapter, "Connecting with Our True Selves," facilitates the reader's ability to identify core values, plan solitude, and set a course for being "found" by his or her Mighty Purpose.

DREAMRUNNING STRATEGIES

. . . .

Expertise in each of the three Noetic Practices evolves through the *dreamrunning* strategies presented in this book, called Recipes for the Sole. Ten strategies facilitate mastery of each practice; these are listed on the following page.

NP 1	NP 2	NP 3
Dreaming the World	*Reframing Experience*	*Playing with Time*

• Game Board	• Breathpull	• Just to There
• Tipsy	• River	• Effect/Cause
• Snapshots	• Tow Rope	• Mainspring
• Mirror World	• Giant Hand	• SloMo
• Visualizing Sensations	• Skyhook	• Remember Now
• Unthing	• Just Yours	• Frames
• Zooming	• Shado Pull	• Rush Point
• Being All	• Life Line	• Rockabye
• Sourcing	• Inner Listen	• Falling
• Turning the Globe	• Mother	• Running into the Past

HOW IMPORTANT ARE THE RECIPES?

. . . .

I have been asked, "Isn't it enough just to read the book and try to practice the techniques without running?" My answer is, *It depends.* On the one hand, you can't build those intuition muscles just by reading about "Being Run." *Dreamrunning* is like any purposeful system of self-change: whether it be weight loss, financial management, or learning a musical instrument, you must practice to experience its benefits and achieve mastery.

Dreamrunning involves choosing to engage the will on two separate levels. On one level is the decision to take on the noetic discipline of changing ourselves from the inside out. On another level is a commitment to put the Recipes for the Sole to use in everyday life without worrying about what happens. This means having faith that in the long run this *in vivo* practice will train our unconscious in flexibility, free up the mechanisms that control our beliefs and attitudes, and help us become masters of our own reality. And so, it is in the use of the Recipes where it all comes together, out there wherever the path of today or tomorrow takes you. The Recipes are the dream-inducers and the strength builders.

On the other hand, it's not necessary, or perhaps even advisable, to *run*—at least to run in the way that term is normally held these days in the public consciousness. All-out athletic running is a high-impact activity—fine for some, but stressful, unpleasant, and potentially injurious for others. Most importantly for our purposes, the performance aspect of the sport known as "jogging" may be downright antithetical to producing the mental and spiritual results we are seeking. Running in public causes the ego to kick in (How do I look?), and *dreamrunning* is a process of bypassing the ego. It can also be practiced while walking, swimming, biking, or using a treadmill or exercycle.

WUN-RALK

. . . .

What I recommend is an ideal exercise for using the Recipes, which does not tire or injure, and seems to be easy and fun for everyone. The pace is a bit more than a walk, yet just short of a run. Since the term "run-walk" is already used in sport magazines to mean alternating between periods of running and walking, I've chosen (at the risk of sounding like Elmer Fudd) to call this pace the *wun-ralk*. The upper body moves as in running—arms bent and swinging to lift the body slightly on each step—while the lower body moves as in walking—heels planting instead of striking. The measure of this activity is that the head, instead of bobbing up and down, moves forward in a straight line. Anyone, old or young, athletic or not, can find great joy and great inner strength and peace by building the habit of going out and *wun-ralking* through the Recipes.

Dreamrunning is for everybody. Whether you exercise or not, whether you are a manager, a teacher, a homemaker, a software designer, a retail sales clerk, a top corporate executive, or an auto mechanic, *What's the Rush?* can train you to get balance into your life. As we approach the millennium, the minds of more and more people are bewildered and their thinking is narrowed by coping with the horrendous amounts of change that they encounter. *Dreamrunning* can help train the mind to deal with so much change.

As this activity continues to be a source of continual joy for me, I am convinced that it can activate the capacity to experience the abundant bliss that lies within each one of us. That is the real reason that has impelled me, after all this time, to gather the Recipes for the Sole, the strategies for inducing the *dreamrunning* experiences, into this book. In place of the bitter brew of everyday, humdrum, business-as-usual existence, I offer the challenge of tasting for one moment the elixir which *dreamrunning* offers—exercises to change our minds to keep up with the times.

Some authors start by telling you how to read their books. I won't presume to do that. For me, a good book is like a good run. It may start off clunky and slow, the mind resisting until the body warms up and starts humming along, but it gathers momentum, and at the finish there is that indescribably warm, wonderful sense of having earned something worthwhile and important. My only tip is that, since *dreamrunning* is about "being run," you might use the same principle. That is, instead of reading the book (i.e., wrestling with the concepts and efforting at grasping every detail) just "be read." That is, give up control and let the book read you. Enjoy the ride!

—*James Ballard*
Amherst, Massachusetts

CHAPTER 1

On the Run

Only that day dawns
To which we are awake.

Henry David Thoreau

A: "Got a minute? I need to run something by you."

B: "Well, okay, but I'm really running late."

A: "This will only take a second. Could you run by the market tonight?"

B: "Sure. Just fax me the list. Hey, I gotta run!"

A: "Catch you later. I'm on the run myself."

Running is an apt term for the frantic pace most people maintain in these times. Life has speeded up, and many of us are not sure how it happened or when we bought into it. Are we running after something? from something? or just running to keep up? It may not be clear where we're headed, but we are clearly in a hurry to get there.

It reminds me of the pilot and navigator who are night-flying through a thick fog.

Pilot:	What's our position?
Navigator:	I've got good news and bad news.
Pilot:	What's the bad news?
Navigator:	We're off course and hopelessly lost.
Pilot:	What's the good news?
Navigator:	We're making excellent time.

Lots of individuals and organizations today, if the truth be known, are exactly like the hapless fliers in this dialogue: they are lost, but making good time. While they struggle to close the gap between the way things were done in the past and the way they need to be done now, the pace of change is fast outstripping their ability to deal with it. In an effort to just keep up, people carry lengthy to-do lists and intricate planners; they enroll in more and more sophisticated time-management courses. In an effort to compete, companies are downsizing, flattening, rightsizing, restructuring, and re-engineering. Amidst all this activity, few if any concentrate on the real crux of the problem—the matter of *changing our minds.*

We are living faster, but still thinking at the same old rate. The peculiarly "Western" overemphasis on rational and logical thinking, which has enabled us to advance so far in the field of technology, threatens to run us into the ground. The dilemma of coping with a constantly changing world forces us to focus on our own psychological and spiritual states and compels us to learn ways not only to manage them but transform them.

The Recipes for the Sole offer enjoyable ways to practice shifting one's belief structures (notions of what is going on) at will. They are a set of tools for altering reality—for conscious dreaming, if you will. The idea in *dreamrunning* is to go out each day for a walk or run, plug in one or another of the Recipes, and spend a short time in a fascinating version of reality that you personally create.

"It sounds like fun, but I don't even have time to do the really important things I have to do." Sound like anyone you know? Pay strict attention, for here we encounter precisely the conundrum that prevents so many people from getting off the treadmill their lives have become. They'd like to solve the issue of "not enough time"—but they don't have time! When life is moving faster, is there a greater need or a lesser need for reflection? Greater. When life is moving faster, is there more time or less time for reflection? Less. The world will not give you this critical time to reflect on where you are going and whether or not it makes sense. You must carve it out for yourself. The core need for many of us is the need to *spend time with ourselves.* The *dreamrunning* routine begins by forcing this discipline, then helping to ensure it.

The rationale behind this book is more than whimsical. *What's the Rush?* promises a far greater benefit than making a run or a stroll around the park more fun. It fosters a process of restoring balance to life. Specifically:

- balancing logic with intuition
- balancing attention on the present with attention on the future
- balancing control with surrender
- balancing thinking with feeling

Why embark on a program like this of refitting our minds? And why *now,* when most people say they don't have time for exercise or for any additional demands? To understand and appreciate the reasons why living successfully at the close of the 20th century requires us to undertake a radical reconstruction of our thinking and behavior, it's helpful to look at a brief history of change, and explore the way in which change itself has changed.

HOW CHANGE HAPPENS

. . . .

The accelerated pace of life over the last few decades has deeply altered the character of our lives. This change in velocity has occurred most dramatically during the last three decades and has come about through the information explosion. People acquire information faster, and this has produced an imperative to stay current, to have constant access to the latest data. Before 1990 the idea of a person's maintaining a home phone, an office phone, a car phone, a portable phone, a beeper, a fax machine, and access to e-mail and voice-mail would not have been believed; today's on-the-go business people feel they need all this.

The steady acceleration of change has brought us to an Age of Uncertainty. Some people are paralyzed by so much change, and react by running faster and faster just to keep up. Unfortunately, there is no end in sight to the running. To understand how *dream-running* can train us to replace these coping modes and recover our joy in daily living, let's examine briefly what has happened to us and how the world has come to feel so confusing.

There was a time when a change came as an interruption to a more or less normal state of calmness and stability. The change messed things up for awhile, but when it was over you were able to settle back into a comparatively stable state. Such a change might be depicted as an S-shaped curve like the one below.

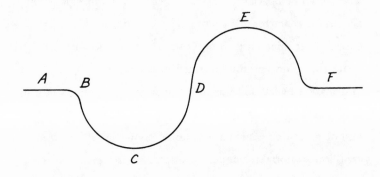

A = prior period of stability

B = unfreezing of old systems*

C = low point of disruption, confusion, loss, depression

D = period of implementing change

E = refreezing of systems into new order

F = return to stable state

* Psychologist Kurt Lewin invented the terms *unfreezing* and *refreezing* to describe change.

To illustrate, let us use an experience common to most people, that of moving. The period of stability represented by the left-handed flat line (A) in Figure 4 stands for the time lived in one's residence. Once the decision to move is reached (often abruptly these days because of sudden transfers and other upheavals), the household begins to come apart (unfreezing of the old system). The line in our diagram descends (B) because the place is in sudden pandemonium; as belongings come out of closets, basements, drawers, garage, and attic, it no longer feels like home. Coping with all this upheaval is confusing and disorienting; research suggests that moving is one of the major stressors in life, right up there with job loss, divorce, and death of a loved one.

The bottoming-out of the downward line (C) could represent the point at which everything is packed up and on its way to the new domicile. From here to the top of the S-shaped curve is implementation (D)—the effort involved in making the move actually happen. Point E marks the settling in to the new domicile. This not only involves unpacking but also settling into a new community, with parents acclimating themselves to new jobs and children to new schools. Finally, familiarity develops and we are over the upheaval—things are refrozen into a new order. Soon (perhaps within a matter of months) the sense of stability returns (F).

Similar illustrations of the change model can be made using the learning of a new skill or technology, or becoming accustomed to the loss of a loved one or valued friend. The interruption that this change makes on the screen of stability can be shown this way:

However, now that we've explained how a change is an interruption to stability, we must acknowledge that things no longer happen that way. The freezing/unfreezing model was fine for the 1950s when Lewin contrived it, but it's far from descriptive of the times we live in.

A CHANGE IN CHANGE

In terms of frequency of change, such a rarely interrupted period of stability was characteristic of the period up through the Fifties. In the Sixties, though, changes began to occur more frequently. The rapid development of information technology—television, computers, communication satellites—resulted in people knowing more things faster.

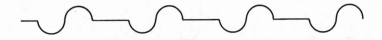

Change, now the norm, was interrupted only briefly by periods of no-change in the Seventies.

By the time we reached the Eighties, change was more or less continuous and becoming a way of life.

These diagrams, stylized and simplistic as they are, portray a steady increase in the velocity of change during the decades of the information explosion.

Change brings the coming apart not only of the way things were but of the way *we* were. The decade of the Nineties has ushered in an unprecedented shift, not only in the velocity of change but in the way people experience it. The stable state, which had once been normal between changes, has disappeared altogether. In the new system, the changes are running into each other, overlapping.

The preceding decades had all along been leading up to this, like some huge silent earthquake in slow motion. People were sensing that their ability to stay in control of their lives was being eroded, but it was happening so gradually that they experienced it only intermittently, as an increase in the rate at which they had to run after things. Typical of our event-conscious society, minds were focused on day-to-day, year-to-year changes—fashions, baseball scores, celebrities, the stock market—rather than on the "big picture."

What is the impact of the overlapping of these changes? Typically, the mind barely begins to focus on the disintegration of an old order before another unfreezing is upon it—and then another and another. The mind, which previously functioned with some certainty, can no longer concentrate on getting a change completed; it must leave it unfinished and rush to attend others. Much of what is called stress is really accumulated frustration from repeated failure to achieve psychological closure.

DEALING WITH UNCERTAINTY

As we approach the new millennium, the interlocking of changes occurs at a faster rate. Finally it becomes a constant, resembling waves in the rapids of a river. We are living in a condition which writer Peter Vaille calls *constant white water*.

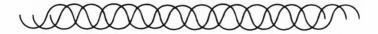

Not only are there more changes, but there is less opportunity to participate in making them. We are suffering from a lack of destiny control. Particularly in corporate life, changes that deeply impact the way people do their work are merely announced, and employees are expected to submit willingly. Having more to do, but having no vote about it, apparently comes with the job territory. To get an idea of how unpredictability operates in your own life, try the following exercise.

Try This Right Now

. . . .

Listing Changes

On paper list at least 5 changes you have recently gone through, are now going through, or are about to go through. Next to each item, place either a star or a downwards arrow. The star indicates that you initiated the change, or at least had a vote in it. The downwards arrow shows that the change was imposed on you. How many stars do you have? How many arrows? What are your feelings about this?

Those of us who grew up in the decades of stability between changes are not "wired up" for so much uncertainty. Stability and predictability are diminished, and yet we still act as if we expect them. The inability to see most tasks through to completion has led large numbers of bright, creative people to adopt an attitude toward life characterized by "settling," concentrating on merely surviving. This kind of mental resignation creates a reliance on *mechanical thinking*—using the mind to proceed superficially through the motions of routine tasks and habituated actions. When mechanical thinking becomes habit, it results in a kind of daily sleepwalking.

How do we acquire the skill of living without expectations? We need tools that allow us to hold a vision of the future lightly in our's mind's eye, ready to be discarded at a moment's notice as conditions shift. Somehow we must transform the expectant mind so as to entertain unpredictability. We must learn a new skill:

Dreamrunner advisory
. . . .

Make uncertainty your friend.

DEALING WITH LOSSES
. . . .

An unacknowledged misery of modern times is the accumulation of losses during change. When we go through repeated changes, we continually give up the familiar. No time for sadness or saying goodbye—things, people, money, benefits, prestige, and the like are simply whisked away. With our attention constantly pointing ahead to anticipate more change, we commonly continue in a coping mode and deny the hurts that attend these losses.

Change brings the loss, first of all, of stability. Without the familiar look and feel of traditional order, one is thrown back to being a beginner. Well-known supports disappear, as do familiar things and people. In the average person's workplace today, he or she typically incurs losses of fellow workers, free time, space, conveniences, prestige, recognition, supervision, and hours off work. What is done with the grief that attends these losses? Where do people put it?

Research by Elisabeth Kübler-Ross and others has shown that the person experiencing loss (particularly a painful loss such as the death of a loved one) passes through a series of more or less predictable "stages" of grief. These stages apply to all kinds of loss—loss of a job, a title, or a career, loss of associates who leave a company, loss of children who mature and move away, loss of privacy and serenity when an aging parent moves in, loss of the familiarity and security when we move to a new location, etc.

. . . .

STAGE 1. *Denial*

The person is in shock, coping outwardly with the altered situation, not yet in touch with his or her actual feelings about it.

STAGE 2. *Anger*

The person is resentful ("Why me?"). The anger may be directed at the agency that imposed the change, or displaced onto others or oneself.

STAGE 3. *Bargaining*

The person tries to recover what has been lost. An example is a child of a divorcing couple, who tries to get mom and dad back together.

STAGE 4. *Depression*

The person mourns the loss. This is the real work of grief; deep feelings arise unexpectedly and threaten to overwhelm the person.

STAGE 5. *Acceptance*

The person completes the work of grief. Having integrated the loss, he or she re-enters life fully.

Try This Right Now

· ·

What Stage Are You In?

Revisit your list of changes. For each change, identify
something you lost or had to give up. These may be tangi-
ble things like money, friends, office space, secretarial help
or child care. Or they may be intangibles like time, feedback, community, or a sense of yourself as being knowl-
edgeable or seen as an expert. Finally, place a 1, 2, 3, 4 or
5 next to each item to indicate what stage of grief you are
in with regard to that loss.

The psychological experience of living in constant white water is
something like passing through scores of these grief stages, su-
perimposed upon each other. Many of the losses people incur are
not serious enough in themselves to be debilitating, but the sheer
number of changes and the attendant losses add up. It is as if an
army is valiantly fighting on despite daily casualties.

Stream of Change

Constant change and constant loss characterize modern life, and we struggle with how to cope. For instance, we have no way to ritualize the passing of what we have lost and commit it to the past as we do through a funeral. With its losses ungrieved and no recovery period available, society can function in cumulative chronic grief, something like a pervasive low-grade fever. People can and do get up each day and go to work, so eventually this state of unconscious mourning becomes business-as-usual. Even though everyone is going through it, they have no ways to get together and talk it over or find remedies for the pain. They smile as they enter their places of work and greet each other as if nothing were happening. This collective denial is commonplace in large business organizations.

Denial takes its toll on the home front as well. Gone are the milk and cookies when kids come home from school; gone the nationally observed "days of rest" when stores were closed and workers' souls as well as their bodies were *off* to relax and be with the family. Nowadays, following a hectic weekend spent shopping and busily catching up on pressing matters at home, many people are glad to return to the relative order and predictability of the workplace!

As changes have intensified, along with the avalanche of information and concomitant shifts in lifestyle described in this chapter, a widespread feeling of being at-risk and powerless has developed. Many people feel exhausted and discouraged by constantly coping with events and circumstances beyond their control. There appears to be no alternative but to scurry faster, trying to keep up with it all. This puts these people in the *littlethink* condition.

In *littlethink* one feels powerless in the tides of change. *Littlethink* results from regarding the world of sense experience as the only reality, time as an increasingly scarce resource, and oneself as at the effect, rather than at the cause, of these implacable forces. *Littlethink* is a flat, dimensionless existence in which one feels trapped in the material world, where one's efforts are never enough, because the only world one perceives consists solely of consumables. The diagram on the next page depicts this state of mind.

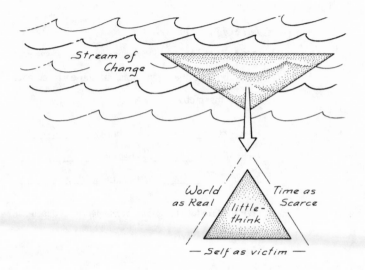

You may be asking: *Well, what good does it do to cry about it? What can you do about it anyway?* At the risk of repeating myself, let me suggest that you can always change your mind. The activity below provides some suggestions.

Try This Right Now

. . . .

Talking to Yourself

STEP 1: Think of a difficult problem you face. On separate paper complete these sentences, making each sentence relate to that problem.

1. I want to _____ but _____.

2. I have to _____ because _____.

3. I can't _____ because _____.

STEP 2: Make the changes in your sentences as directed in the footnote below.

In sentence 1, cross out the word "but" and write "and." In sentence 2, change the word "have" to "choose." In sentence 3, change "can't" to "won't." As you make these changes, what shifts do you feel? Conclusion: One way we can get out of littlethink is to change our self-talk.

During the past few decades we have experienced an acceleration of change, leading to the state of constant white water. However, our minds have not kept pace with these changes; instead of steadily adapting to the changes we have maintained our old ways of perceiving and thinking. We revert to mechanical thinking and form habits of coping rather than creating. We need a new way of responding that allows us the freedom to accommodate uncertainty and recover more rapidly from setbacks and losses. This recovery begins with acknowledging our feelings and our need to reorient our minds for the new millennium.

CHAPTER 2

Escape from Littlethink

> "Use the Force, Luke."
>
> *Obi-Wan Kenobi, in* Star Wars

Dreamrunning puts us in touch with our life purpose, the essence of why each of us is here. If you were to ask the average person on the street, "What is your purpose in life?" he or she might answer, "To make it through until Friday." This is the kind of short-term thinking characteristic of people today. It is certainly one kind of goal, but it is a very narrow and limited one. It is reactive, not proactive. Focused on endurance and survival, it does not open a person up for the possibilities of happiness and fulfillment. As the pace of life speeds up, it becomes more and more essential for us to consciously choose, and continuously re-choose, a personally validating, overarching purpose in our life and work. Within our hectic existence, it's easy to forget that:

Dreamrunner advisory

· ·

The most important thing in life is to decide what the most important thing in life is.

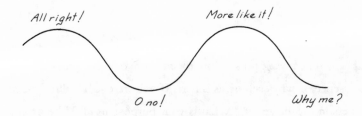

All right!

More like it!

O no!

Why me?

Most people see life as a series of ups and downs: now healthy, now sick; now rich, now poor; now success, now failure; now cold, now hot; now happy, now miserable; now alive, now dead. If we could just get it right! But the undulating wave of life is meant to teach us something, if we'll only listen and pay attention.

First of all, it shows us the folly of being attached—stuck with the way things are, or were, or will be. Detachment from outcome is a consummate skill for being effective in times of continuous change. For, when we hold events (people, places, possessions, opportunities, expected achievements) lightly, we free ourselves from being possessed by them. We become grateful borrowers, contented utilizers of things-temporarily-on-loan. Secondly, we need to realize that we're not trapped in our little vehicle traveling that roller coaster of a ride; we are the space in which it happens. *We are all of it!* The inevitable ups and downs of life do not claim us. Walt Whitman's poem, "Song of Myself," perfectly expresses this detachment from events.

The sickness of one of my folks or of myself, or ill-doing or
    loss or lack of money, or depressions or exaltations,
Battles, the horrors of fratricidal war, the fever of doubtful
    news, the fitful events;
These come to me days and nights and go from me again,
But they are not the Me myself.
Apart from the pulling and hauling stands what I am,
Stands amused, complacent, compassionating, idle, unitary,
Looks down, is erect, or bends an arm on an impalpable
    certain rest,
Looking with side-curved head curious what will come next.

Maintaining this enlarged or "soul" sense of ourselves is absolutely critical for weathering the quick turns that come our way in the rapids of change. We cannot regain this heightened self-regard as long as we are stuck to the notion that we are victims of the changes happening around us. Paradoxically, what frees us into this larger space of detachment is the practice of being contentedly absorbed in what we are doing, with no concern as to the outcome of our action. The *Bhagavad-Gita,* the Hindu Bible, expresses it this way:

> *He that acts in thought of Brahm,*
> *Detaching end from act, with act content,*
> *The world of sense can no more stain his soul.*

THRIVING ON CHANGE

Imagine the following scene taking place in a manufacturing company: Members of a work team have been toiling for months on a project and are just about to finish it. The boss, emerging from a high-level meeting, abruptly announces to the team that the project has been scrapped. They must begin work immediately on a new project which the company's research has shown is more in line with anticipated customer needs. The team members stop, look at each other for a moment—and suddenly break out in wild cheers, slapping each other on the back and talking excitedly about the new project!

For most of us this is a totally absurd scenario. Instead of being elated and ready to embrace the new work, the group would most likely show an immediate loss of morale. Shock would give way to anger, anger to intense regret and suffering from the feeling of loss because of the team's psychological investment in the project and attachment to its outcome. A long period for the team to overcome its disappointment would be needed. For the company, this recovery could be costly. The strategic decision to alter the product design to meet emerging market needs could result in lowered productivity, even loss of key people, largely because of the production team's inability to cope with it. The company's window of opportunity might be lost.

But stop. This is the reaction the workers *would* have had *before* they learned to accustom themselves and their work units to sudden change—before, we might say, they had learned to dance on the rugs being pulled out from under them and learned to enjoy the dance! In short, the unthinkable scenario described above is a picture of people whose mentality has been reconstructed so that they are not just surviving in the steady chaos of the "constant white water" condition—they are thriving in it!

What has enabled these people to be such mental superstars in a world where uncertainty is so certain? The answer is two-fold. First, their work is *values-driven;* providing outstanding service to the customer governs their decisions and actions. Second, they have incorporated each of the three Noetic Practices into their thinking and learned to live in such a way that being happy no longer depends on outer circumstances.

This team has subsumed the practices under one overarching purpose, to the extent that all of their activities are aligned. They are thus empowered to shift their perspective from conditions and circumstances to stay "on purpose" and to move in one continuous direction with laser-like intensity. When a significant change occurs (such as the boss's announcement of the need to drop the project and begin a new one), their perspective enables them to understand this simply as a mid-course correction. It does not touch their inner purpose (that of providing outstanding service to customers) at all; in their view, it is just something that happened along the way.

FINDING PURPOSE THROUGH SURRENDER

The previous example about the work team members who were able to shift gears without costing them or their company a loss of time or energy shows how a shared, values-based mission can drive team behavior. It is an example of how essence overrides form. Behind the stream of chaos we call "constant white water" there lies a wonderful secret: If we are not unnerved by the constant flow of changes, we can be energized by it. We can not only be changed, but renewed and empowered. By ceasing to fight the current and by concentrating on balancing initiative with wise surrendering, we enter a wondrous realm wherein we can view the shifting world from an entirely new perspective. We are fully as active in it as before, but our actions all mean more. What we do *counts*.

Albert Einstein said:

Small is the number of them that see with their own eyes and feel with their own hearts. But it is their strength that will decide whether the human race must relapse into that state of stupor which a deluded multitude appears today to regard as the ideal.

Very few of us know how rich our lives could be if we only used our time wisely. Instead, we squander it by running here and there, mostly at others' beck and call. Constant change causes us to lose our focus; our days go by in a blur, and our actions are reduced to coping mechanisms.

All highly effective people have learned to concentrate, to gather their attention and focus it to a point. When we can first of all identify our most important duties, then perform them with close attention, we achieve economy of motion. Everything except what is in the beam of our attention becomes extraneous, and we enjoy an exhilarating elegance of action. The things we are seeking seem to seek us instead. In that moment, we are *on purpose*.

To be effective and happy in our shifting world, and to escape from the confines of *littlethink,* we must learn to *grok. Grokking* is our capacity to intuit—to simply and deeply *know* something without knowing how we know it. In most people, it is like an unused muscle. We have no idea what we can accomplish with this power because we are so identified with the body and with thinking (processing information brought to us by our five senses). It is as if a machine were designed with an elegant capacity for increasing the mechanical advantage of all of its parts, but the circuits are bypassed and the mechanism continues to clank along in the same old limited way.

For example, the runner whose attention is scattered feels alienated from his environment, rather than in command of it. As soon as the runner occupies his mind with one of the Recipes, his attention becomes focused, and he achieves an immediate economy of motion. He becomes one with the landscape, the running surface, his body, other runners. (I have heard this sense of unity reported by both marathoners and fun-runners).

Imagine for a moment having such proficiency with the Noetic Practices that you can move through each day in the bliss known only to one who is the utter master of self and experience. You would thus be *grokking*—i.e., able at any moment to intuit your experience, and only secondarily relying on the senses and the rational mind to process data.

LIMITING ASSUMPTIONS

. . . .

How do we *grok*? First, by acting as if we can. If we assume that our knowledge is limited by what we can take in through the senses, we're stuck already. The *littlethink* condition is based on limited conceptions regarding the world, the self, and time.

But another source of knowledge exists other than that which is gained from sensory experience. Intuition, or inner knowing, bypasses our rational processes and comes to us all at once. This is what we mean by *grokking*.

To *grok* is to see beyond the appearances that fool ordinary people. In my view, the third century Neoplatonic philosopher Plotinus was discussing *grokking* when he wrote:

External objects present us only with appearances. Concerning them, therefore, we may be said to possess opinion rather than knowledge . . . Our question lies with the ideal reality that exists behind appearance . . . This region of truth is not to be investigated as a thing external to us, and so only imperfectly known. It is within us.

The capacity to *grok* is not something we must add to ourselves, the way we have had to add outside knowledge over the years of study and experience. Each of us already possesses the capacity to *grok*. Hunches, sudden epiphanies, leaps of faith—these are all evidences of a capacity that is there all the time. *This knowing is limited only by our ability to receive it.*

A NEW WAY TO WATCH THINGS HAPPEN

Constant white water, as we've discussed, is an apt metaphor for a world in which, just when you've begun to work on one change, another change hits you. The effective constant-white-water rider disciplines the mind. He or she is able, when the tidal waves of changes are breaking, to calm the mind, pinpoint its attention, and *watch things happen in a new way.* In order to understand the nature of this heightened attention, we can take cues from whitewater enthusiasts, those who enjoy getting into a boat and braving fearsome rapids.

Eric Magneson, a world-class kayaker who tackles some of the fiercest rivers in the world, puts it this way:

> *The moment before you drop into a big rapid, your concentration is absolute. Any fear or doubt there once was, is gone. There's just no room for it. Sitting in a kayak you're only three feet high, and the waves around you are pretty big, so it's really hard to see what's going on. You're trying to pull off a series of precise moves to be in pretty exact spots in the rapid. Time warps. Sometimes it seems to slow and stretch, and things seem crystal clear. Then other times everything's flashing by in fast-forward, and you're just straining to keep it all together. You don't have to think about what your body is doing; it seems to respond instinctively. It's a total mind-body experience.*

This passage describes a relaxed, alert concentration, an ability to see exactly what needs to be done in any certain *now,* without having to know it ahead of time. It suggests a rule for living happily amidst constant change:

Dreamrunner advisory

· ·

Don't fight the current, learn to cooperate with it.

Learning to cooperate with the current of constant change requires detachment. In practical terms, detachment is the ability to enjoy and to do good work without being linked psychologically and emotionally to its outcomes. Detachment enables us to cooperate with the swift current of change. It is at the heart of mastering constant white water because it is essentially the ability to *concentrate while letting go*. It is paradox in action.

WHEN TO DIP THE PADDLE

· ·

Understanding how a kayak is maneuvered in white water illustrates how to deal with the waves of constant change. The kayaker cooperates with the current by keeping the boat pointing downstream and uses the paddle to make minute directional adjustments to keep the boat ends parallel with the flow.

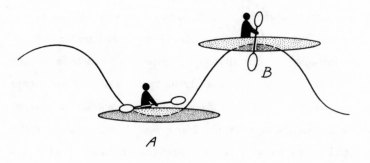

The diagram above illustrates two situations in which whitewater paddlers constantly find themselves. When the paddler is in a trough between waves and the boat ends are in the water (A), it is futile and exhausting to try to use the paddle. On the other hand, while the boat is high on the crest of a wave and its ends are out of the water (B), even a little paddling can make a lot of difference. Therefore the rule is:

Dreamrunner advisory

. . . .

Dip on the crest.

The expert kayaker relaxes when he or she can make no difference with the paddle and spends that time watching for the next opportunity to exert strategic advantage. We can translate this "dipping on the crest" rule of kayaking into a strategy for dealing with white water change: *When you can't make a difference, relax and observe, ready to leverage the flow when you can.* These days, due to the quick restructuring responses companies are making to keep up with changes in markets, customers, and competition, many people find themselves "between jobs." Unfortunately, this causes stress, worry, guilt, and anxiety. They tell themselves: "Something is very wrong here. This shouldn't have happened to me. I should have a job, *now!*" This mental punishment prevents their effectiveness in job-hunting, causing them to be less creative in problem solving, less confident during job interviews, etc. If they stopped fighting the current and relaxed, they might see this time as an opportunity to explore new possibilities, such as starting a new career or business, moving to another location, or staying home while their mate works. In other words, they might be empowered by *letting* things happen, rather than *making* things happen.

The diagram below suggests how the "dipping on the crest" rule might play out.

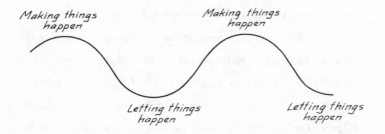

Making things happen

Making things happen

Letting things happen

Letting things happen

Eric Magneson's kayaking description alludes to the fluid nature of time when one is so absorbed. *(Time warps. Sometimes it seems to slow and stretch.)* This corresponds with many athletes' descriptions of being "in the zone," when they have all the time they need for executing a normally difficult maneuver. The adept *dreamrunner,* whose practice has enabled him or her to *grok,* learns to be "in the zone" more of the time than out of it.

SUMMARY

· ·

Dealing with constant change in the *littlethink* condition of hopeless, random coping not only steals the balance and joy from life but its meaning and purpose as well. A program of self-change, like *dreamrunning,* with its deliberate shifting of perceived reality can reconnect us with our deepest selves, our souls, and return us to the joy of serving our core purpose. *Dreamrunning* develops the intuition, allowing us to transcend the flat sensory world and to live more by intuitive perception, or *grokking*. It takes concentrated practice to attune ourselves to widen our neural receptivity and *grok*. The next three chapters present actual techniques which you can begin to use immediately to achieve these results.

CHAPTER 3

Dreaming the World

There is a difference between one and another hour of life, in their authority and subsequent effect. Our faith comes in moments; our vice is habitual. Yet there is a depth in those brief moments which constrains us to ascribe more reality to them than to all other experiences.

Ralph Waldo Emerson, "The Over Soul"

When people talk about the most real moments in their lives, they often say, "It was as if time stood still," or, "I felt as if I were in a dream." Are they, in effect, saying that the unreal is truly the real? For me, such moments are timeless. The moment blooms open. I am at one with whatever is happening, feeling graced and fortunate, absolutely convinced that my place in the lifeboat is assured. Whenever I have experienced this dreamlike consciousness, I've had the hunch that I was closer to what was real, and that most of what people call "real life" was actually unreal. This conviction has followed me throughout life. You can discover this wonder—whether or not you are running, walking, or practicing any other vehicle for the Recipes—when you *practice seeing the world as a dream.*

This first Noetic Practice and its relation to the NP pyramid is shown again below. Use of this Practice enables a person to lift his/her consciousness above the troubled waters of change. The empty space at the top represents the new perspective the user achieves, which enlarges with continued use of the Practice.

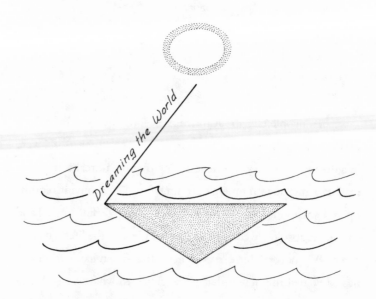

· ·

As a little child, I was utterly convinced that life was a dream. Each morning I opened my young eyes upon a fascinating dreamscape, and as I went out to play it was with the anticipation of a fresh surreal adventure. Soon, however, I made a painful discovery: my perceptions of the nature of existence were not shared by others. The conversations and actions I observed with family and friends made it clear that they considered material existence as the only reality. Faced with the fact that I did not "make sense" of things the way others did, I kept my beliefs to myself. For a long time I inwardly validated my private sense that things were somehow essentially unreal. However, as I grew up and as tasks and responsibilities increased, the dream state of being began to fade. As happens in the growing-up process, the mundane nature of existence began to occupy my consciousness. Without realizing it, I became bogged down in making a living rather than making a life.

ISLAND DREAMS

· ·

Some years ago I had a unique opportunity to put my perceptions about the true nature of reality to the test. I was working on a book about the psychological aspects of running (which turned out to be the earliest version of this book), when a friend who owned a house on Martha's Vineyard offered to have me house-sit the place in the off season. On a warm September afternoon I found myself on the ferry boat, journeying to an island retreat to write a book. As I watched the sun reflecting in millions of wink-ing diamonds on the vast smooth surface of the ocean, it seemed that a dream of good fortune had surely come true. Then and there I decided that I would studiously practice thinking of my time on the island as a dream. In this place of removal from the "mainland" of human thought, where I knew nobody and no-body knew me, I would test out my lifelong premise.

At first it seemed that my experiment in "dreaming" my island existence was merely indulging a whim, but it soon began to pro-duce interesting results. I quickly found that the act of casting away my socially conforming mental restraints, and acting outright as if everything were a dream, was changing me. This is not to say that my outward behavior was bizarre; anyone observing me would have seen a "normal" person (perhaps smiling to himself often in a cryptic way). Because I regarded the details of each event in a new way, I paid greater attention to them, feeling that sense of wonder which one ascribes to a surreal dream-happening.

Far from dulling my enjoyment of life, the deliberate practice of seeing the world as a dream made me more responsive and alive than ever. My perceptions were quickened and intensified; my "dream" experiences seemed more real than before. Dreaming my hours and days kept my attention in the present moment; this acted to mitigate moods and soften little attachments and disappointments. After all, if everything were happening in a dream, things "mattered" only relatively.

As I continued my experiment, each day came to resemble a magical world wherein divine serendipity ruled. Breakfasting at a coffee shop, I would be entertained by a whole series of dreamlike happenstances. Some overheard fragment of an islander's conversation would coincide with a thought I'd had upon awakening. The very phrase I was writing in my journal would drift to me from a song on the cook's radio. The waitress, as I was about to order pancakes, would say, "Pancakes today?" Or I would return home to find an unexpected phone message from someone I had planned to contact that day. I began to be convinced that I was a player in a pre-arranged drama in which all things were simply going through their motions at the behest of some hidden stage manager.

The more I practiced viewing mundane events as dreams, the more convinced I became that I was seeing them for what they really were. The sensory world was shifting to resemble the dream I was hypothesizing it to be. A hidden life breathed from behind all things. I was revisiting the daydreamland of my childhood. It is impossible to convey the wonder and joyous confirmation I felt upon discovering this.

DREAMRUNNING

It was inevitable that my perceptual shift would affect my writing and running. My research laboratory for the book became the four- to six-mile run I took along the seashore each morning. One day on a long, boring run, I began to imagine that it was not my will power and muscle that were making me run, but that my breath was pulling me forward. As I immersed my mind in this thought, all the usual physical strain of running—plus the self-induced stress that comes from wondering how long or how far I'd run, or any worry about how I might look to others—simply vanished. It was as if, instead of running, I was *being run*.

In succeeding runs I generated other relaxing mind games, which I came to think of as "recipes" for transforming the running experience. Using them required concentration at first. (The mind can be scandalized by the notion of skewing its carefully nurtured version of "reality.") Then invariably, the exhilarating shift into the effortless, timeless feeling that I called *dreamrunning* would emerge.

In looking back over my journal entries, I found that my new habit of seeing the world as a dream was allowing me to tune into hidden resources within myself. My writing was improving, the work blossoming out in new and unexpected dimensions. Many profound realizations came to me about myself, as well as novel ideas and solutions to problems I was experiencing. By the time I left the island I had concluded that, even though most people might not see the use of viewing the world as a dream, I could heartily recommend it as a way to be happy, induce creativity, and live rewardingly without the pain of attachment to outcomes. *Dreamrunning* had enriched my life.

Some readers may ask: Isn't this business of "dreaming" life really just passivity, a handy means of escaping responsibility? My answer is that the difference in taking life as a dream rather than as an ultimately serious business is not in action but in attitude. It is not what one does that is transformed, but how one experiences the doing of it. Recognizing the dream nature of life opens one's heart up to the romance and spirituality of being alive; when this happens, the pursuit and fulfillment of one's responsibilities take their rightful place. One regards them lightly, rather than as burdens.

In addition to the freedom from stress and anxiety that dreaming the world provides, there is empirical evidence that would support our following the advice of a popular bumper sticker: *Question Reality.* When we regard the world as a dream, we come close to the view espoused by the modern quantum physicist. Demonstrations conducted in particle physics substantiate the fact that what we perceive as solid matter is not solid at all. Rather, what seems so solid—the earth we walk upon, the objects we handle, the food we ingest, these very bodies with which we are so identified—are in reality little more than shimmering spaces of vibrating energy, frozen into the forms we recognize.

Theoretical physicists are well aware of the surrealistic nature of the world. In the early 1930s the ultimate constituents of matter were believed to be protons and neutrons (constituting the atom's nucleus) and the revolving electrons (constituting its outer shell). Since then hundreds of elementary particles have been identified, some of them with very short, others with almost unlimited life spans. Many of these particles act very strangely. M. Gell-Mann, who received the Nobel Prize in 1969 for his discovery of a particle called the omega minus, suggested that these elementary particles consist of yet more elementary entities called *quarks.* With each succeeding dissection of these whirling particles into smaller ones, and with the realization that most of so-called solid matter is simply space, science approaches the amazing possibility that *there's nothing there without our thinking it's there.*

One of India's most eminent scientists, physicist J. C. Bose, said, "All creative scientists know that the true laboratory is the mind, where behind illusions they uncover the laws of truth." Immanuel Kant (1724–1804) said that time and space are not real objects of the external world but ideal, internal creations of the mind. Like a machine that acts upon raw materials to make a finished product, the mind acts upon its sensory impressions to fashion its experience. In no sense, according to Kant, are laws of physics like time and space inherent in nature; they are only modes of thought we use to shape our interpretation of phenomena. The mind of man takes whatever content it receives (through its own precepts and concepts), then reproduces what it believes to be reality. "The world is my representation," Kant wrote.

Decades ago the dual personality of the electron, partaking of the characteristic of both a particle and a wave, led Sir James Jeans to observe, in *The Mysterious Universe:* "The stream of knowledge is heading toward a non-mechanical reality; the universe begins to look more like a great thought than like a great machine."

Sir Arthur Stanley Eddington likewise observed, in *The Nature of the Physical World,* "The frank realization that physical science is concerned with a world of shadows is one of the most significant advances . . . It is all symbolic, and as a symbol the physicist leaves it. Then comes the alchemist Mind who transmutes the symbols . . . To put the conclusion crudely, the stuff of the world is mind-stuff."

Statements like this remind me of a spring day when I was in the fifth grade and my teacher, Miss Holman, was discussing molecules. She was comparing the action of electrons whirling around the atomic nucleus to the movements of planets orbiting around the sun. As we went out to recess, my mind was zooming between macrocosmic and microcosmic dimensions. My friend John Gallagher and I threw ourselves down on a grassy bank at the side of the playground and gazed up into the blue reaches of sky, quietly ruminating on the lesson. Then came a defining moment for me. John said, "What if this whole world is just a bunch of atoms in the dream of a huge giant?" The bell rang and we went inside, but I was oblivious to all that happened the rest of that afternoon. I felt like Robinson Crusoe when, believing himself to be utterly alone on his island, he came across a fresh human footprint in the sand.

The ancient writings of India declare that the universe is a dream of God. Paramahansa Yogananda employs the art of metaphor to correlate this idea with the findings of physicists. In his *Autobiography of a Yogi,* the great master compares the universe to a movie:

> *Just as cinematic images appear to be real but are only combinations of light and shade, so is the universal variety of delusive seeming. The planetary spheres, with their countless forms of life, are naught but figures in a cosmic motion picture. Temporarily true to man's five sense perceptions, the transitory scenes are cast on the screen of human consciousness by the infinite creative beam.*

Yogananda states that the smallest particle of matter, undiscernible by any physical instrument, is the "lifetron." What he calls "thought-trons" are the bridge between lifetrons and the force projecting the dream-universe. He calls life "a dream within a dream," for within the universe (which is the dream of God) each person is thinking and moving within the dream of his or her own consciousness.

Yogananda's metaphysical explanation makes practical sense

to me. It verifies the harmony and consistency of the objective world. At the same time it assigns each of us a role in the "cosmic movie," a role each person dreams separately. Diversity within unity, the very model of nature, is the secret of our conscious experience.

WHO IS RUNNING THE SHOW?

. . . .

Like the dream nature of the world, the intimation that we are not the "doers" of our own actions is based far more on fact than on fantasy. How much of our life do we really "do" and how much is "done through" us? Let us consider thinking itself. Like dreams, our thoughts come to us unbidden. To verify this, stop reading and practice:

Try This Right Now

. . . .

Watching the Thoughtstream

Sit quietly for 2 minutes with eyes closed. As if you are observing the mind of another person, watch the flow of thoughts as they come up. Concentrate. Remain detached.

Likewise, other processes we think of as "ours"—breathing, heartbeat, circulation, digestion, the body's immune system—proceed as unconscious processes. What makes them all go? I choose, as many have done down through the ages, to call this agency *life force*. It is life force, acting through us, that makes our lives "happen."

But, some may argue, actions are different. They are the result of the will. True enough, the will is engaged when we walk, talk, eat, write, and perform the myriad tasks of the day. We want to put will at the source because it is the conscious part of acting. We reason, then will, then act. To us, thinking about doing an action and doing it are so linked in our experience, they hardly seem separate. But the neuro-physiologist will tell us that the signaling process in the brain, nervous system, and muscles which activates movement is quite complex—and that it all occurs well beneath our conscious awareness.

Who, then, is the real "doer" of what we do? It is the life force again. The will seems to be the originator because we are conscious of it, and we know our action would not occur without our willing it, but the will is actually the tool of the life force. The life force, we might say, acts *through* our will to run the body, to get things done. (We realize this truth sometimes through hindsight when we say, after an experience has passed which we had questioned or resisted at the time, that it "had to happen" or "was for the best.") Thus, "Being Run" does not represent a thing of fancy, it is the actual truth. When, through the use of the Recipes, we imagine ourselves "Being Run," and induce the feeling of "Being Run," we bring to conscious awareness what is already going on.

Lest anyone imagine I am suggesting that some alien force has invaded and we have become helpless robots, I hasten to state that we must reconceptualize ourselves, not as the body but *as part of the life force.* Our identification with the body is the cause of all our problems, for it is based on illusion. *Dreamrunning* is a way to get back to identifying with the real you, part and parcel of the lifeforce, divine essence. As before, I call upon you to test this for yourself:

Try This Right Now

. . . .

Being One with the Life Force

For the next few minutes practice the consciousness that you are the life force. Think: *I am not this body. I am not this mind. I am a part of That which animates the mind to think and the body to move.*

The rational, linear mind is a useful servant, but a poor master. C. G. Jung once said, "Rationality is the superstition of the twentieth century." As that century draws to a close, our reliance on a purely rational, linear mode of thinking is being tested. The forces of change are driving us to develop new, instantaneous ways of knowing. Recent work on multiple intelligences, and in particular the research and writings of Daniel Goleman, Ph.D., author of the book *Emotional Intelligence,* has shown that each of us has available a variety of ways of knowing. White water change makes it incumbent upon us to pursue and leverage the enormous advantages which these modes offer.

SUMMARY

. . . .

In this chapter we have explored the dream nature of the universe from a variety of perspectives—my own discovery of *dreamrunning,* that of science, and by means of exercises you can try yourself. The truth is that the universe *is* a dream, and many wonderful and practical benefits await us when we begin responding to it as such. Most importantly, the sense of victimhood, so pervasive during these pressured times, is dissipated when one grasps the essential truth that reality is of her or his own making. Consciously dreaming the world makes every event assume a merely relative significance, and restores to the individual the lost art of not taking life so seriously. While releasing the self from attachments, it restores a mythical, larger-than-life aspect to existence, within which each day is truly an adventure.

Dreaming the World

. . . .

Breath Pull

As you run,

suggest to your mind that you are not

the one doing the running.

Your breath is sucking you forward. You are

being vacuumed forward, breathed forward.

Relax, concentrate on this idea

and enjoy the ride.

foot-notes

. . . .

Lock in the Breath Pull for sixty breaths. (If
you lose concentration, begin counting over
again.) Feel the lightness in every step, in every cell, as you are whisked forward, not of
your own accord.

If you pay strict attention, you might even
notice how the running speeds up a little bit
each time you inhale.

recipe for the sole

. . . .

River

Pretend that you are
not moving forward at all,
that you are actually
standing still.
The surface you run on is
moving toward you
and under your feet.

foot-notes

· ·

In this constantly changing world, it seems that nothing lasts. But something does last—You. Not your body. We're talking about the Real You, the part of you that endures.

Recipes like *River* afford practice in being that Real You by building the perception that material life is just stage scenery passing by.

. . . .

Skyhook

Feel your running body hung in air,
legs turning like a windmill,
while again and again the earth below
takes a breath, rising to cushion
your footfall, then descending.
Watch the earth's breast rise and fall
with each step, bouncing you playfully
like a parent with a baby.

foot-notes

. . . .

What relief to let go—if only for a moment—of the tedious "normal"! The weary
mind rejoices, delights, become childlike
again—*sees!* It's a homecoming, like being
returned to your native country after being
gone an unbearably long time.

. . . .

Game Board

Imagine one of those toys you tip and turn
to roll a tiny ball through a maze.
Now see the landscape you are running
through as the game board and
yourself as the ball.
You are running because the Giant
who is manipulating the world is
tipping the board.
When you make a turn, it's because
the Giant tips the board
in that direction.

foot-notes

· ·

Play this same game with the "Giant" of
Unexpected Turns of Events. When something happens that others might call a "set-
back" or a "reversal," deliberately cast a net
of ownership around that event. Your constant white water mantra should be:

Just what I wanted!

recipe for the sole

. . . .

Tipsy

As you mount a hill,
pretend that you are really running downhill.
See the top of the hill
as the edge of a cliff
you are approaching.

As you are going down the other side,
pretend you are running uphill.

foot-notes

· ·

Gravity is another of our agreements—a useful one, I'll admit, and one you don't want to tamper with much. The word gravity also means *seriousness*. There's no reason to be grim or "heavy" about things. (As stress consultant Loretta LaRoche says: "A wet towel on the bed is not the same as a mugging.") Being too grave leads—well, just there. This Recipe, like others, tricks the mind away from business-as-usual. When that happens, you *lighten up*.

. . . .

Snapshots

Run with eyes closed,
blinking them open
every few footfalls or so
to glimpse the way ahead.

Relax, and concentrate
on the closed-eye times.

foot-notes

. . . .

For this Recipe, pick out a wide, smooth field, a straight stretch of untrafficked back-road, or a broad, hard-packed beach. You might discover that concentrating on the closed-eye periods makes your run most relaxing and exhilarating. It's like running and meditating at the same time.

You might come in from a 4-mile run, having run only about a mile of it with your eyes open.

You might get hooked on this.

· ·

Mirror World

An exact replica of yourself
is running upside down below you.
The bottoms of this person's feet
are touching yours at every footfall.
The surroundings of that mirror person
look just like yours,
only in reverse.
Now switch and
become that mirror person.

foot-notes

. . . .

Holding the mind in an alternate reality as in *Mirror World,* even for a few seconds at a time, develops the greatest of all powers— the power of your own mind. The ties of civilization, those bonds of social convention and conformity that exact so much of our attention, do nothing for us. Fears, worries, and unhappiness result from a life uncontrolled by wisdom. It's time to retrace our footsteps Home to the divine freedom we are all seeking. Before you finish using this Recipe, transfer all fears and worries to that mirror person.

recipe for the sole

. . . .

Visualizing Sensations

Whenever you feel pain,

concentrate on it.

Make it be a shape, a color.

Are the edges blurred or smooth?

How much water would it hold?

Is it making any sound?

foot-notes

· ·

Try this visualizing technique next time you have a headache. Sit down, relax, close your eyes, and visualize your headache. Ask the questions in the Recipe. The reason it works is that *what you resist, persists*.

Many headaches are made up of resistance to having them. By focusing on your hurt, you remove all your resistance, so the pain starts to diminish. Try this with other "aches and pains" of life. For instance, see what happens when you pay lots of attention to someone who's a "pain."

Unthing

As you move along, set your mind to see

not things, but unthings—

spaces where things are not,

shapes of air around and between objects.

Sense a kind of connective tissue—

an ether, if you will—

lying just outside the data ranges of the senses.

An invisible glue binding

all of us "things"

and our fortunes together.

foot-notes

· ·

Wherever you are reading this, stop and listen to the sounds around you. Bring one sound to the forefront of your attention and concentrate on it for a few moments. Then release it and isolate on another sound from another source. Practice pinpointing your listening for a while. Then, release the sounds entirely, and focus instead on the silences between them. (A new way to listen: when someone is speaking, concentrate on the spaces between his or her words.)

. . . .

Zooming

As you run,
look down on the details of the
running surface as if from a great height.
Imagine that you are a Giant,
gazing down upon a tiny world
where a tiny ant-size runner
appears far below.
Then switch and be that runner,
sensing behind and overhead
the vast Giant of yourself,
studying that little you
from beyond the clouds.

foot-notes

. . . .

If you get the zooming from giant self to ant-size self and back again going in a rhythm (say, switching from one to the other every 12 footfalls), you can create a running laboratory to study relativity.

- How do you find balance in your life?
- What moments are most precious to you?
- When does time go away for you?
- When do you experience the peace of giving up and letting go?
- When do you feel the most like yourself?
- What is happening when things seem sacred, elemental to you?

. . . .

Turning the Globe

As you run,

create a picture of yourself from space.

There you are,

running on top of that blue ball of the earth,

turning it with your feet

as you hang

motionless in space.

foot-notes

. . . .

Getting out of *littlethink* requires that we expand our consciousness. Look for opportunities to cultivate the feeling of expansion. Expand your mind right now to room size ... building size ... town or city size ... planet size.

Sometimes we cheat ourselves by running after things, playing the game of Get More Stuff. Truth is, all possessions of the earth, no matter how great they may be, are limited compared to what is already ours. With the world as our birthright, all this acquiring behavior is a little like a prince or princess messing around in a dumpster.

recipe for the sole

. . . .

Being All

Imagine each bit of information
brought to you through the senses
as occurring inside you.
Expand to include all sounds,
sights, and smells.
Put your running form inside,
and the surroundings in which it runs.
Concentrate on this,
until nothing that happens is
outside of yourself.

foot-notes

· ·

Erase the difference between what is you and what isn't. The mind might ask, "Why would you want to practice this?" Answer: To jiggle yourself out of your movie—the script that time-worn habit seems to dictate you observe.

Wouldn't it be odd if a movie actor got so "into" his part that, when the script called for him to be shot, he actually died? That's not far from what we do every day, when we attach ourselves to these seemingly scripted roles we play.

Telling yourself: *I really* am *this person, of this age, with these habits and identifying marks, living at this zip code on this date,* etc. is the essence of limiting your being. Unlock this little piece of the *littlethink* puzzle. Don't be determined by the past, or even by expectations of the future. Forget these role confines and ask: "Who *might* I be?"

recipe for the sole

· ·

Sourcing

Deliberately choose to act as if
you are making it all up.
See and feel everything "out there"
as originating within you.
As the environment changes, create
felt linkages between its shapes, colors,
temperatures, textures and events
and your own
shifting inner landscape.

foot-notes

· ·

Life in the meatgrinder of change can be a killer if you spend even a short time of it hiding out in dull routines. Break out. Blow the whistle on the real enemies: conformity, mediocrity, vulgarity. Shut it down and speak out for quality of life. Be a projector watching its own movie. Create the world by noticing it. It's all in your mind, anyway.

CHAPTER 4

Reframing Experience

> The greatest discovery in our generation is that human
> beings, by changing the inner attitudes of their minds,
> can change the outer aspects of their lives.
>
> *William Blake*

These days, each one of us is required to go on a hero's journey. Constant white water change causes us to leave home—our comfort zone of habit, our addiction to the way things have been—and sets us on a journey where the perils are not so much physical as psychological and emotional. We can become lost and wander in the dark forest of circumstances and trials. Our minds can cower before the fierce dragons of worries and concerns that threaten to overwhelm us. We have, however, been given a talisman—the ability to transform the situation by seeing it in a new way and acting toward it as if it *is* that way. As we learn to use this magic tool we find the power to break the spell of powerlessness, wanting, and discouragement. This magic talisman is Noetic Practice Number 2: *reframing experience.*

The project of training our minds to operate efficiently and happily in the new century begins with applying a basic principle:

Dreamrunner advisory

. . . .

Consciousness is the only game in town.

This means that consciousness is not what we see but what we see *with*. You and I may witness the same event, but we don't see it the same. You see it through the experiences and assumptions you bring to your seeing, and I see it through what I bring to mine.

Five people crossed a meadow together. The real-estate developer used the stroll to scan for a possible building project. The scientist studied the geologic formation of the landform. The lover was preoccupied with composing a sonnet to his sweetheart. The teacher prepared a field-trip lesson for having students identify wildflowers and insects. And the child spent all his time trying to catch a butterfly. Did they see the same meadow?

The nature of perception is to be selective. No one can perceive every aspect of a thing or event. Attention is like a searchlight, illuminating the thing it is pointed at, and leaving all the rest dark. This means that whenever we perceive anything, our attention is always selecting out points about it to notice—without our noticing that it is doing so. You can conduct an interesting experiment with your own attention:

Try This Right Now

. . . .

Paying Attention to Your Attention

Take a piece of paper and a pencil and sit quietly for 2 minutes, observing and noting down whenever your attention shifts. As soon as the searchlight of your attention shifts to a new object—sensation, thought, memory, etc.—write down what it shifts to. (Example: *bird song . . . memory of brother . . . itch . . . computer hum . . . TV show . . . breath . . . cat rubbing leg,* etc.)

Since what we select to notice becomes the totality of the event for us, in that moment that is all there is—what we see is what we get.

So what? What does all this about the nature of perception mean for us in practical terms? It means that, as Yogananda said when he spoke of human consciousness being a "dream within a dream," each of us is in a sort of waking dream. We are awake in that our sensory nerves and brain are doing their job of keeping us on track in the world, but we are dreaming our point of view— only seeing what we see and not aware of what we are seeing *with*. We are dreaming because we are assuming that the way we are seeing it is the way it really is. In terms of the impact of this fact on the quality of our daily experience, there's good news and there's bad news. The bad news is that as change continues to accelerate, our consciousness can solidify, holding us more and more within the stressful confines of *littlethink*. The good news is that we can wake up by realizing we're dreaming, and change the way we see things. Since we are authoring the dream (by seeing it in the unique, selective way each of us sees it), we can change it (by seeing it in a new way).

What makes two people select different aspects of the same event to notice? One answer might be that they've had different experiences. Past events are a key to the real selectors shaping what they highlight, but more importantly it is the beliefs, expectations and attitudes they've adopted, based on decisions they have made, based on those different experiences.

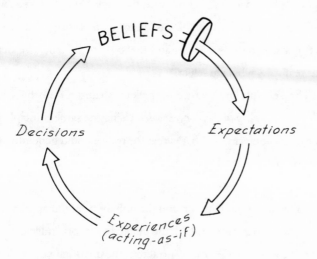

The diagram above suggests that our beliefs (which are based on decisions we made, formed from our experiences) become a lens through which we see the world. We then *expect* those beliefs to be fulfilled, and when we *act as if* what we believe is so . . . we prove it so! Beliefs, then, act as self-fulfilling prophecies.

Perhaps you have heard the saying, *Argue for your limitations, and you get to keep them.* Let's look at an example. A person has a belief that people will not like him so he acts that way—keeping a distance, avoiding eye contact, etc. People, seeing this, do not approach this individual. His mind can then verify its belief. *(See, I told you!)* Thus we always find what we are looking for—i.e., what we believe is there. Our beliefs direct us to those facts in each event which reinforce them and make them be true. We define our reality by what we select.

The self-fulfilling nature of beliefs is captured in the saying: *The rich get richer and the poor get poorer.* Using the same principle that our beliefs determine what is real for us, we could generate other versions of this:

- The happy get happier, and the unhappy get unhappier.
- The liked get more liked, the unliked get more unliked.
- The attractive get more attractive, the unattractive get more so.

In order to change our perceptions, we must work at the level of our *beliefs* (i.e., what we think is so), for they are the real selectors. Since we made these beliefs up in the first place (or, bought into them if they resulted from the influence of others), it follows that we can change them. Once we do, our experience (including our behavior response) changes automatically.

A friend of mind, a single mother, told me recently how she used *dreamrunning* to improve a situation with her teenage daughter. Helen was thinking about how to confront her daughter, Annie, about her low grades and lack of effort in school. The longer she thought about the problem, the more angry and confused she became. She decided to go for a run to cool off before her daughter came home from school. Soon after starting her run, she practiced the Recipe called *Tow Rope*. While running she relaxed and concentrated, temporarily convincing her mind that instead of running she was being pulled forward by an invisible rope. By suspending disbelief in this way, Helen began to feel the actual sensations of being pulled gently down the road. "As I practiced Being Run," she said, "the effort and stress I'd been feeling just slipped away. I felt I could run for hours."

Returning home, Helen found that the feeling of surrender

and calm was still with her. "When Annie came home, we sat down and I went through the interaction with her in a calm, watchful way. Instead of encountering the usual resistance, I found her receptive. As the conversation unfolded, it seemed that Annie and I were partners in something that was 'doing us.' I was able not only to make my own needs known but to listen and understand her feelings as well. Annie told me she wasn't happy with her grades, either. She agreed to improve, and we made a schedule for regular homework time, with coaching from me as needed. That discussion not only solved a problem, it deepened our relationship." Helen's story illustrates the very practical benefits that often occur from *dreamrunning* practice.

Most of us have had the experience of shifting our beliefs. You meet someone and immediately dislike him, yet in time, given the continuing impressions that come with further association, you find that you like him. The shifting of beliefs can sometimes be done much more quickly, deliberately, and consciously.

The fact is, this discussion of belief-shifting represents a wake-up call: It is reminding you that the plot of the life-drama you're starring in has shifted. It's a constant white water world and you can't afford to maintain the way you've always looked at things. Fortunately, you can rewrite the play by changing your assumptions.

The analogy of play writing is useful here. Imagine an author who writes a play with a "surprise script." It is cleverly contrived so that when it is staged, the action proceeds for awhile as planned, but at a certain point the actors are surprised by a minor unexpected event or announcement. Each actor copes in his or her own way with this; they then proceed on course until another aberration hits, and they are thrown again. As deviations from the rehearsed script begin to happen more frequently, and as cast members realize that their old scripts have less and less application to what happens on stage, they begin to react in different ways. Some ignore the scenario changes and try to keep things in place by repeating their old lines as if nothing had happened. Others, paralyzed by the uncertainty and not knowing how to cope with it, stand around and hope it will go away. Yet another group finds the situation fascinating and begins to study how they can fit into it. They maintain their roles in the play and make up lines to go along with the plot changes. As the play proceeds, they begin to re-shape their roles as necessary and to improvise their lines. These improvisers become more practiced at their new craft; while speaking and moving around on stage, they look for the next surprise so they may adapt their role accordingly. In time they forget the old way of following their assigned roles and begin to enjoy being a creative part of a living, evolving drama.

When the play ends, these actors seek for and play out other "living" roles. In fact, they decide not to return to the old way of rote acting; the risk taking and creativity inherent in the new way are far too compelling.

The Recipes for the Sole provide a training ground for becoming such actors upon the changing stage of life, where we seem to be at the beck and call of a hidden Stage Manager. The Recipes help us develop one of the most useful skills we can have in making change our friend—the skill of *reframing*.

WHAT IS REFRAMING?

To reframe something means to change the way you experience it, without changing the thing itself. To understand how reframing works, examine the following picture.

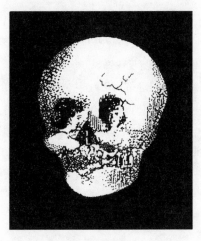

All Is Vanity

At first glance, you might see a skull. Upon closer examination, you may identify a lady at her boudoir. When you switch from seeing one to seeing the other, you are using the skill of *reframing*. In this process you are shifting your conceptual-emotional viewpoint and placing the situation into another "frame" which fits the situation as well or even better. The concrete facts of the situation remain the same, but you have shifted its meaning.

Why is this ability to reframe a situation so important to living in a constant white water world? Because the world you see today is like the weather in New England—if you don't like it, just stick around and it will change. Reframing can keep us from getting stuck in the way things just were.

Using the reframing skill to shift the meaning of a picture shows that you already possess the mental skill of changing the meaning of an event at will. In a larger sense, you have demonstrated the ability to use an elegant principle for effectiveness in constant white water:

Dreamrunner advisory

. . . .

Change the way you see the world, and change the world.

Now, look back at the "All Is Vanity" picture and practice shifting back and forth between the skull and the lady, so you can get a clear sense of what reframing—changing the meaning of the picture at will—"feels" like in your mind. Now focus only on the skull. Think what you would feel and do if that skull were actually physically in your presence. What would you feel toward it—repugnance, curiosity, fear, depression? What would you do in relation to it—move away, lean back, utter an expression of disgust? Now, reframe the "All Is Vanity" picture so that you see only the lady. What would you feel if the young lady were in your presence? Interest? Curiosity? Friendliness? Would you greet her? Move toward her?

In each separate situation, even as you were imagining it, you can see that each separate "framing" of the situation (skull or lady) induced an altogether separate and unique emotional and behavioral response. And therein lies the creative power of our ability to reframe: *when you change the way you perceive a situation, you automatically change the way you feel and behave toward it.*

REFRAMING CONTRIBUTES TO HAPPINESS

The reframing skill does not serve you if you feel unable to use it in certain situations where your view of things seems fixed and determined. Your willingness and ability to create new meaning out of the old facts of your situation—without the facts themselves having to change at all—become critical when used to make yourself happy. Satisfaction in life often depends upon your ability to see opportunity where there seems to be nothing but chaos, to see good where evil predominates, to look behind the actions of others so as to understand them rather than judge them.

I once lived in an apartment complex in a college town that was occupied by a number of students. There were occasional loud parties, and sometimes an altercation would occur in the parking lot outside my window. One night I was awakened by a young female, obviously inebriated, delivering threats and obscenities at the top of her lungs at one of her girlfriends. Immediately my mind started in with its judgments: *How can people make noise like that this late at night? Where do girls learn this kind of disgusting language? Why don't parents raise their kids better?* In the midst of this outrage, I suddenly stopped blaming and started listening to the actual content of her outburst. Between loud threats of bodily harm, punctuated by swearwords, were phrases like, "And don't you forget it! What makes you think you can get away with that with me—huh, missy?" Suddenly it was clear to me that this young person was unleashing a torrent of words from her own past. As if she'd punched the replay button on a tape recorder in her head, she was replaying messages that had once threatened and frightened her. Speculating about whether this girl had grown up listening to a bullying parent I suddenly felt completely accepting of her behavior. Things soon quieted down outside, but as I reflected on the reframing that had occurred in my consciousness I imagined "before and after" scenarios of what I would have done, had I acted upon each of those two sets of perceptions.

Initially, when I was stuck in blame, I imagined going to the window and yelling at the girl, telling her she had some nerve screaming that way when people were sleeping, threatening to call the police, etc. After reframing the situation with understanding and compassion, however, I saw myself going outside, casually walking up to this person in the midst of her tantrum, and waiting until she had stopped and looked questioningly at me. Without a word I motioned to her silently to come with me over to a bench at the side of the parking lot. She followed me, and smiling, I said, "Sit down here a minute with me." My calmness had an effect on her, and she complied. We sat there for a full two minutes without saying a word. Her breathing quieted and she relaxed. Finally, I looked over at her as if to say, "Okay now?" She nodded, thanked me, and rejoined her friends. Even though this scene had occurred in my imagination, it struck me as a logical way I would have responded to my shift in perspective.

This simple skill of reframing, which we all can do, can become an invincible weapon for fighting and winning the battle of life. It empowers individuals and organizations to rise above their circumstances, to achieve productivity and satisfaction in a world which others see as hopelessly random and unpredictable. *Dreamrunning,* simply stated, is training in reframing. As such, it helps us learn mind magic—using the same facts to verify a new possibility. With continued practice of the Recipe techniques, the mind becomes accustomed to shifting its reality at will. Gradually, it relinquishes its habituated "one way" of seeing the world, and perception becomes more fluid.

Once we know the trick of reframing, we can apply it deliberately to our everyday experiences. Reframing means working with our feelings and attitudes as well as our ideas. We can use this tool whenever we feel any hint of stress or unhappiness. For example, we can reframe any situation:

- from boring to *interesting*
- from difficult to *easy*
- from unrewarding to *fascinating*
- from frightening to *fun*
- from discouraging to *hopeful*
- from too fast, slow, cold, hot, hard, easy, plain, fancy, whatever to *just right*
- from frightening to *curious*
- from stressing to *relaxing*
- from the wrong boss, parents, spouse, workmates, kids, neighbors to the *right* ones

The following story may suggest a way to use reframing events to preserve balance.

All the people in the village envied Farmer Ben because he owned a horse. "You're so lucky!" they said.

"Perhaps," he said.

One day the horse ran away. "Too bad," the villagers said.

"Perhaps," said Ben.

Soon the horse returned, leading another wild horse. "Now you have two horses," they said. "How fortunate!"

"Perhaps," said Farmer Ben.

In trying to ride the wild horse, his son was thrown and broke his leg. "Pity!" said friends.

"Perhaps."

When army conscriptors came through the village, taking away young men for battle, they passed up the ailing boy. "Do you have good luck, Ben, or what?" the people exclaimed.

"Perhaps," replied Farmer Ben quietly.

HERO'S JOURNEY

. . . .

"I have imagined a life," wrote Walt Whitman, "which should be that of the average man in average circumstances, and still grand, heroic." Throughout time, certain gifted individuals have managed to derive happiness and to experience well-being, right in the midst of adversity. These persons see the very conditions that overwhelm others as opportunities. They refuse to become disillusioned or cynical, or to allow their behavior to be determined by these conditions. These people earn our admiration; they occupy the central roles in our "feel-good" movies and stories. Their accounts stand in strongly stated contrast to the tiresome "news" of everyday crime, dangers, and scandals. These implacable optimists are our modern day examples of a myth that has endured in every time and place in human history; they represent the myth of the Hero's Journey.

The Hero's Journey begins symbolically with the hero's leaving home; sometimes he or she is thrust out by circumstances. Hardship (which nowadays could be the loss of one's job, a loved one, or health) sets the hero on his or her mythical journey of self-development. Along the way the person encounters great odds; in the old stories this was typically a place of great danger or a fearsome enemy. Sometimes the hero was given a talisman—a charm or magic weapon that would help him or her to do battle with the dark force. By facing these trials, by overcoming fear, weakness, or attachment, the person became a conqueror.

Nowadays, accessing joy amidst adverse conditions is clearly the responsibility of us all. Like it or not, we must all become our own heroes. How do we do this? A rule of fiction writing is: "The hero is the one who changes." We become heroes by *changing our minds,* by purposely altering the way we see things. "I hate being frightened," wrote Captain Joshua Slocum, who circumnavigated the globe alone several times in a small sloop, "but even more I detest being prevented by fright."

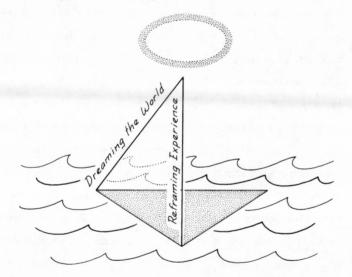

The diagram above shows how use of the second Noetic Practice of Reframing Experience in combination with the first, Dreaming the World, broadens the user's perspective (represented by the widened space at the apex).

A particularly potent place to start our practice of reframing, in order to fit us for success in constant white water, is with the nature of life itself. In the age-old dispute between the optimists and the pessimists, the question seems to be: *Who is right?*

The answer, of course, is that both are "right," in that each can point to facts to corroborate his or her position. But now the question comes (and not unreasonably, given the constant white water nature of things, where attitude is all important to success): *Who is having more fun?* The indisputable answer is, the optimist. The world of the happy person is in fact quite a different world from that of the unhappy one. In either case, the person has not only a predilection but an actual *determination* to see things as he or she understands them.

An example of this determination is that of explorer Richard Byrd, who ordered his men to leave him alone in a hut hollowed out of the Arctic tundra to take weather readings throughout an entire winter. Seeing the sun set for the last time for the long winter, Byrd wrote in his diary:

> *The sun peeped above the horizon at noon, and with that hasty gesture set for the last time. 'If you hadn't lost the sun,' I told myself, you*

would have had something serious to think about, since that would mean that the earth's axis was pointing the wrong way, and the entire solar system was running amok.

The iron rule of perception—that you are bound to get what you are expecting—means that inevitably the optimist will attract more positive experiences, and the pessimist will attract more negative experiences. The optimist acts out his or her commitment to being happy by looking for ways to be joyful even in the midst of troubles. One rule which applies to every constant white water surfer's advantage was suggested by the lovable comedian Fred Allen, whose sardonic radio persona belied the fact that he was a committed optimist. Allen was fond of saying:

Dreamrunner advisory
. . . .

If you always want what you have, you always have what you want.

The person of "ferocious optimism" practices contentment with the way things are, while in the very act of trying to change them for the better.

The practice of militant optimism is never more needed and more powerful than in difficult times. Constant white water provides an ideal time to build these new mental muscles by acknowledging that "If life gives you lemons, make lemonade." Katherine Hepburn, in the voice narration of her book *Me,* relates the choice to meet life squarely and amicably back to the ability of human beings to dream:

> *We read fairy tales for years, don't we? Are they throwing all that out? If you don't dream up your parents, your brother, your sister, your friends, the person you love—if you can't dream them up, if you just see them as total-4-letter-word "reality"—then God help you. You've got to dream up everything. I believe in miracles. I believe that here we are, and we can be in severe physical trouble, but if our spirits aren't in severe physical trouble, then we can rise up out of it. That's what we've got that all the animals haven't got.*

Understanding how consciousness works—i.e., how beliefs guide our perceptions to produce the experiences unique to each of us—can empower us to examine some of our basic notions and attitudes about ourselves, others, and the world, and to change them accordingly. The skill of reframing becomes a particularly powerful tool for building effectiveness in constant white water. Reframing can literally make us the masters of our experience, especially when we use it to transform apparently negative events into opportunities for growth.

Reframing Experience

. . . .

Giant Hand

As you run up a hill,
feel a Giant Hand
cradling your body and
gently pushing you
up the slope.

foot-notes

. . . .

What if a great, resounding Joy—abundance in every sense—lay always within us, waiting to be accessed, and we didn't know it?

What if the answers to all our needs, the fulfillment of all our dreams, were trembling on the brink of being discovered, and we were deaf and blind to them? This and the other Recipes can open the door to those inner riches.

You might find, as I have, that as you crest the hill, the Hand switches to the front of you, and gently cradles you as you "fall" down the hill.

recipe for the sole

. . . .

Just Yours

Run backwards,

leap, swing arms high,

shuffle along with

one foot leading the way.

Skip. Dance to an inner tune.

Make your run be

Just Yours.

foot-notes

· ·

When you run, you need not conform to some marathoner model. Defy tradition. Flout convention. Fancy up your stepping—make it a tap-dance, a pirouette, a top-hat-and-cane shuffle.

Own the landscape you run in. On a flat, deserted road run down the centerline. Surround a police station. Gallop through sunshine in a cemetery.

recipe for the sole

. . . .

Shado-Pull

Run with the sun

low and at your back.

Study the long shadow

of the running figure

that stretches ahead of you.

Then *grok* that it is the real runner;

you are the shadow.

foot-notes

. . . .

Study that shadow-self, until you feel with Peter Pan—that *it* is doing *you*. It's amazing how easy things are, when your shadow is doing the work.

Later, catch your shadow winking at you as it pulls you through the day.

recipe for the sole

. . . .

Tow Rope

Let yourself feel pulled ahead
by an invisible rope
attached to your chest.
Someone is reeling you in.

foot-notes

. . . .

Capacity for surrender has not been an ad-
mired trait in western society. It implies
weakness and seems to violate the sense
we have inherited from our forebears that
the world is to be conquered.

Perhaps this tendency to conquer and
control makes sense when man seeks mere
survival, but when it's not balanced with
a letting-go/giving-up/bowing-down, it
leads to exhaustion, dissipation of energy,
and defeat.

Introduce the energy of an *alert surrender*
into your routine of exercise, and open up
whole new worlds.

. . . .

Inner Listen

Let your body tell you

when, where, how, and how long to run.

Feel it out.

Trust your intuition.

Act found,

as if the body always knows.

Listen to your cells.

Tune in to your mechanism.

When does it want to go slow or fast,

leap or lope, gallop, sprint, or dance?

Feel the Flow.

foot-notes

. . . .

Intuition, or deep knowing, should always be trusted. Nancy Rosanoff, author of *Intuition Workout,* identifies three intuitive styles: mental, emotional, and kinesthetic, or physical. Mental intuitives receive messages from the Intuition through hunches. Emotional intuitives decide based on how they feel. Kinesthetic intuitives will feel "comfortable" or "uncomfortable" about something.

Learn what style is yours, and learn to tune in, opening all your receptors to your own Deep Knower.

recipe for the sole

. . . .

Mother

With every footfall,
feel your connection
with Mother Earth.
Feel yourself returning energy
through the sole,
giving back
some of what you've taken.

foot-notes

· ·

The world would have us think in "either-or," separating everything out into particles of them-and-us and mine-and-yours. Every day we need to experience the relief of re-discovering that it's ALL ONE.

Amidst all the whining around us, we undergo healing when we feel appreciation and gratefulness. Besides, research shows that those who practice thanksgiving get more.

. . . .

Lifeline

Whenever your body
raises resistance
or protests at the start of a run,
facing a hill or doing another mile,
shoot an invisible grappling hook
out of your chest, trailing a line.
Feel it land fifty yards ahead;
then relax and let it winch you forward
without strain.

f o o t - n o t e s

. . . .

Your Mighty Purpose is your lifeline. Nothing out there in the world is going to hold you fast; you need an inner anchor.

Your purpose holds your compass steady right through the chaos. Just because you change the way you do things doesn't mean you have to change what you stand for. The way to surmount all obstacles that occur is to *think through them*. Throw your mind out there beyond them, to where you visualize your goal so well that you are never out of touch with it.

CHAPTER 5

Playing with Time

> We shall not cease from exploration
>
> And the end of all our exploring
>
> Will be to arrive where we started
>
> And know the place for the first time.
>
> *T. S. Eliot*

When I was a kid, my mother would sometimes say to me as I was on my way out to play, "What are you going to do today?" I would be utterly stumped. It was a perfectly reasonable question for her to ask a child, but for me it came completely out of left field. My mother would see that my mind was flummoxed and would gently chide me about being a dreamer. Why couldn't I answer her? Where was I *at?*

The reason my mother's question didn't register was that it referred to the anticipated future, while my mind was completely in the place I call the Exact Present. The Exact Present is, more often than not, where kids live—that is, until they un-become kids. To a child who lives totally in the present, anticipation is like a foreign language. When my mom asked me the question, she was *future-minding*. She was speaking in an alien code to her child who was *present-minding*. With enough awareness I might have said, "What do you mean, 'What am I going to do today?' I have no idea. If I knew, what would be the point of going out? I'd stay home." (Of course, I didn't have such faith in my own mentality to have replied that way. Besides, I'd have gotten smacked.)

Similarly, when I returned home after a day of play I would often be faced with another confusing parental query: "What did you do today?" This time my mind, which had been on the present all day long, was being asked to make a sudden U-turn. Again, I would be utterly thrown. *Past-minding*, or reflecting on the past, is another customary activity of the adult mind, but less so of a young child.

RESPONSE-ABILITY

. . . .

The important thing, of course, is not whether you're past-minding or future-minding, but whether you're mentally flexible and can instantaneously wake yourself up, realize where your mind is, and change it. If you live always in the present—or never in the present—progress can easily come to a standstill. The ability to switch modes of consciousness quickly and easily provides the person experiencing lots of change with "response-ability," the ability to respond appropriately.

It's not hard to understand why, in any given moment, the average adult's mind is stuck in either the future or the past. Folks hit the floor running every morning, maintain a killing work pace all day long, and fall exhausted into bed at night—only to awake the next morning after a few hours of fitful sleep and start the whole rat race all over again. Throughout much of this activity, the mind resembles that of a nervous driver in traffic—peering ahead for danger or checking the rear view mirror to see what's happening behind. Talk about being *absent-minded*. The result of so many accumulated hours of future-minding (anticipating what's going to happen, setting up expectations) or past-minding (recalling former mistakes or dangers and using them to act cautiously in the present) is that through all this practice the mind *trains itself not to be present*.

When we consider the quality of work done by the absent-minded person, the cost of being constantly gone from the present moment becomes clear. The elegance of the rational mind consists of its ability to focus through the senses, make inferences about the information, and act appropriately. Organizations today insist, and rightfully so, that their employees have their full attention on their tasks. But how can the future-minding or past-minding person give 100 percent of his or her attention to the present situation? How can he or she concentrate on a present decision, or produce a novel idea for solving a problem? It can't be done. On the other hand, *the mind that operates from the Exact Present expands time.* It is calm, focused, functioning perfectly, and much can be efficiently accomplished in a surprisingly short duration.

DANGERS OF FUTURE-MINDING

Future-minding, in particular, pins us down by attaching us to outcomes. We are not being with what we are doing because we are seeing it only in terms of what it is getting us, what will be ours when we achieve the ends we are working toward. Without some purposeful activity, the mind of the typical runner will frequently leave the present moment and visit the future—the end of the run or the finish of the race. One reason I started to develop the Recipes for the Sole was that I noticed the increase in stress and unpleasantness every time this future-minding happened. As soon as my mind vacated where I was "at" and skipped to the end of the run, the time or distance to there seemed exponentially increased. This not only made that portion of the run unenjoyable, it stole energy from the activity—each time I went to the future, I made myself tired! If that happens in running, why not in other activities? Conclusion: *attachment to outcome produces stress.*

Americans tend to be very goal-oriented, very bottomline in their thinking—and very proud of it. Goals are important, but obsession with achieving them causes many of us to run ahead of ourselves, and to deny the fullest investment of our energy and attention to what we are doing. When we do this, two things happen: (1) we lose the satisfaction inherent in just doing the activity; (2) we help ensure that when we achieve the goal, we will not be around to enjoy it—we'll already be preoccupied with another goal. In sum, we perpetuate *littlethink* experience.

Extremely goal-driven people should not pass off this need for present attention as irresponsible thinking that can sidetrack them from their goals. *Dreamrunning* has everything to do with effectiveness, productivity, and efficiency. It trains us to concentrate (the real secret of all real achievement), and to condense our activities in order to accomplish goals more quickly and efficiently.

Through *dreamrunning* the stresses and distractions of future-minding can be replaced with a sort of double vision—the elegant, if paradoxical, habit of keeping the major portion of one's attention trained on the present (for focused work), while maintaining alertness toward the future (for readiness to change).

REGAINING MEANING

People today might be hard pressed to remember, but it was not so long ago that most things we did seemed to have meaning and purpose to them. Life was stitched together by a series of small, seemingly insignificant events that were their own reward.

Growing up in the Forties and Fifties, I had the privilege (then unappreciated but now missed terribly) of participating in "village consciousness." I not only knew the kids in my neighborhood by name but also their parents, the gas station attendant, the minister, the librarian, and the shopkeepers. A cozy sense of belonging pervaded my world. Things and people stayed the same; they were where you could expect to find them. The neighborhood and the town were my extended family.

Along with this sense of predictability and order went a keenly felt responsibility. I was just as accountable to act well, contribute to others, and stay out of trouble to Mr. Kidston at Kidston's Hardware, or to the pretty, gracious lady with the withered arm who ran the bookstore, as I was to my own parents. Everywhere I went, everywhere I looked, it was made plain to me that I had a role to play in the small drama of our town. That plan, I knew, was part of a larger drama—a Big Story called America. There were things wrong in that story, but the story was there, ongoing, and the job was to work those wrong things out.

Somewhere along the way, things started to get out of balance. It wasn't due simply to the process of my growing up. As a people we started to lose our consciousness of the journey. Whereas once life was clearly a process of fun and entertainment (wherein it was the journey itself we paid attention to and the destination was somehow benevolently foreordained), suddenly the destination became all that mattered. Today it seems that people desire only results. *Being* somewhere—having time to focus on what you are doing, knowing that you are adding value through the doing of it—is sacrificed to *getting* somewhere. Times haven't changed that much, really. The rule is still that:

Dreamrunner advisory
. . . .

When you enter the Exact Present, you expand time.

Any explanation I could offer for the truth of this principle would be inadequate, because language (except, perhaps, the language of poetry) is tied to time. I have asked many people, "When does time go away for you?" and they are always able to respond immediately. The delightful instances they share have the resounding ring of reality to them. Perhaps the real definition of raw, firsthand experience (the kind small children possess) is that which does not occur within what we call time at all. At least it is not sensed that way. Consider the experience of being in love. Some rare individuals have this every moment—they call it *living*. It might be for a single moment that you enter the Exact Present, but that moment is more memorable to you than hours of "in time" experience. Perfectly ordinary things occur, but you are in love with the moment, so they are not ordinary at all.

People nowadays are consumed with "time management," but a far greater need is for righting lives that are out of balance. Loss of time attends loss of balance. The only cure for this anxious sense of rush, this overpowering need to *get* there that pervades every area of life today is commitment to maintaining fundamental balance in our lives.

As the worlds of work and family life are dominated by goals, so is the world of fitness. Instead of recognizing that exercise is a journey to be enjoyed—a pleasuring of nerves and muscles, a relishing of the sensations of the body, a reveling in physical energy and vitalization—people are running endurance contests with exercise machines, counting, measuring, making entries on charts of how many leg-lifts, how much time on the treadmill, and so on.

OUTWITTING THE STOP CLOCK

· ·

Luckily for me, I started my goal-less form of running about ten years before the fitness boom hit in the early Eighties. Nonetheless, over the years I've endured a good many interrogations from people who associate running with keeping score.

"Hey-y-y, I understand you're a runner!"

"Uh-huh."

"So, tell me, how far do you run?"

"I don't know."

"Then, how long do you run?"

"I don't know."

"Hmm. How fast do you run?"

"I don't know that, either."

(Silence.)

"Well, nice talking to you. Gotta run."

The characteristic American insistence on bottomline outcomes is nowhere more evident than in sports. The fields of sport and exercise are dominated by statistics—scores, averages, times, records, calories, pounds, muscle size—all ruled by scorecards, stopwatches, speedometers, pedometers, exercise machine meters, and bathroom scales. It seems that being a sports fan means being a technician.

As we've seen, looking forward to results can rob us of the enjoyment in what we're doing. Paradoxically, our very fascination with measuring distance, endurance, or speed removes the potential enjoyment to be had from exercising. The person who dwells on numbers sees exercise not as something to be enjoyed for its own sake, but merely as a means to an end. Exercise has value only as it contributes to some future point in time. And so the mind leaves the present (where all power and enjoyment are to be had) and settles for the anxiety of some numerical reward that likely won't be any fun anyway, because the journey there has been so unpleasant.

Runners with their minds on numbers know all about this burden. The mind of the typical distance runner teems with fret, a steady stream of bothersome, misery-inducing questions to burden the mind, rob it of energy, deaden its enjoyment:

How long have I been doing this?

Wonder how many miles I've run?

How much farther to go?

How's my heart rate?

How many calories am I burning?

How do I look? Is my form good?

When will this be over?

The connection is rarely made between these self-evaluating concerns and the discomfort of the run, but whenever you reduce running or any other exercise to a program to be monitored and evaluated, you automatically squeeze most of the juice out of it. It becomes work (we call it "working out"). No pain, no gain. We watch the clock and other meters. The pain reinforces the attachment to outcome, and vice versa; exercising becomes a boring, repetitive drudgery, a burden. When it is done this way, exercise is no release from the daily battle of life, it's just more of it. The unfortunate thing is, many of us go at living and working this way. When life becomes a workout, no wonder it's exhausting!

There is a way to completely transform the experience of exercise, to make it enjoyable and rewarding. Clearly, we can not return to life in the Forties; constant white water has seen to that. And few, including myself, would want to do so. There were a lot of things wrong with those times, too. However, we can, if we choose, learn to recapture that storied sense of the age we live in, that vivid everyday romance that once permeated all of existence with magic and super-technicolor, and made us feel a part of something important. Through *dreamrunning* practice, we can begin purposely to transform ordinary life from a petty pace into a fascinating adventure.

THE POWER OF SURPRISE
. . . .

Recently I was running and saw what looked like a small block of wood or stone on the path. I went to kick it out of the way, but when I swung my foot and struck it, I felt no impact at all. It turned out to be a piece of dark-colored styrofoam, practically weightless. The surprise resulting from the discrepancy between what my mind expected to happen and what actually happened woke me up. What would it be like if adults were to arrange things so as to induce a constantly occurring series of discrepant events? My hunch is that if we could do this we would be approximating the mind of a little child. Young children have few expectations; they've not been around long enough to form the habit.

Surprise always connects us with the Exact Present. Its capacity to bring us to the here-and-now bears exploring. A surprise, by definition, is *not what we expect*. Many of the events in the constant white water context which defeat and exhaust people are what they describe as "disappointments." What is a disappointing experience? It is a time when something we expected to happen failed to happen. When we are disappointed, we're rarely aware of the fact that somewhere back there we set ourselves up for this by *starting to expect*. Research shows that you can't be disappointed unless you're expecting something. Stop the expecting, and you cut the disappointment off at the root. *Stop expecting*.

We discount our experience (i.e., make it of no importance) when we expect it, and then instead of being with it, spend our time assessing whether it does or does not measure up to our mental pictures of it. In either case, we've missed *having* the experience because we've forgotten an extremely important principle of physics:

Dreamrunner advisory

. . . .

Wherever you go, there you are.

People's tendency not to be "where they are" is the reason many sages refer to the normal, waking state of consciousness as a kind of sleepwalking. People are walking around, asleep to what is in front of them. Instead of seeing it, they are seeing the idea of it that they brought with them. Many are going through life just checking to see that each thing is there where they knew it would be, or else being surprised that it is not.

Of course, nobody can go through years of life without being awakened once in a while. Moments of sudden surprise, insight, or transcendence are stimuli to the waking-up process. So are moments of impending danger. But we hardly need careen a car over a cliff and plummet toward our deaths in order to witness everything with spectacular clarity. Through the practice of *dreamrunning* we can bring our receptors to the Exact Present.

If, as Immanuel Kant concluded, our experience of time is a subjective one, why should not this ability to be in the flow—to *perceive outside of time*—be available to us always? Why, in our day-to-day lives, cannot we be free of the maddening constraints of "too little time"?

The answer is that we can. *Dreamrunning* is a way to practice this, to perfect our ability to play around with time. When, by focusing in the Exact Present, we master this ability, we experience true timelessness, even while performing our duties and meeting our obligations and deadlines. The moment blooms out, expanding both our capacity to create through our activity and our blissful enjoyment of it. We are in "timeless time."

If by eternity is understood not endless temporal duration but timelessness, then he lives eternally who lives in the present.

Ludwig Wittgenstein

Some readers will ask: What about goals? What about plans and strategies, missions and purposes? Does living in the present mean we just throw our planners aside, forget all our appointments and deadlines?

The answer is: Of course not. You will still be doing each of these things in some present moment. Being fully *there* with, having complete attention on, your planning and goal-setting and strategizing, is what real present-minding is all about.

Dreamrunning teaches us that each moment contains all the time in the world. When we find ourselves in the Exact Present, we are guests at a psychic banquet, invited to do or sample anything we want. We're suddenly stronger, wiser, more caring and more effective. So, lighten up. Declare your independence of the clock to its face. Make time your servant, not your boss. Then you'll be engaging with Noetic Practice 3: Playing with Time.

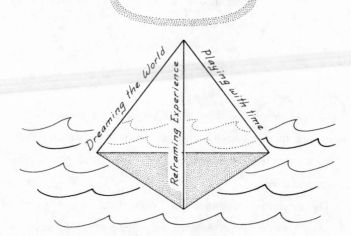

This diagram shows the addition of the third Noetic Practice, Playing with Time, in combination with the other two practices. The perspective from above the "floor" of the immediate experience of change is further broadened. It is this widened view from above that enables us to recognize right action and choose it.

SUMMARY

. . . .

This chapter has described a new place to live—the Exact Present. The present moment generates power and awareness, for it is where everything happens. The more we live in it, the more we see that time is a resource, not a taskmaster. Playing with Time requires detachment, the willingness to release the past and future and *just be here*. For many people this is not only difficult, it is inconceivable. But *dreamrunning* can train us in a new way to watch things happen, to enjoy life from the vantage point of time-abundance, and to perceive right action in the moment.

Playing
with Time

. . . .

Frames

As you run, imagine that
you are in a motion picture.
Each tiny fraction of your body's
forward movement
is captured in a "frame"
of movie film.
Run to occupy each
successive frame.

foot-notes

· ·

Motion pictures often portray a critical scene in slow motion, keying in to the dream-like experience most people have had, of time seeming to slow down or speed up. Were we to think deeply enough about our own time-distortion experiences, we would discern for ourselves that Kant was right when he said that time is not an experience, but the mind's way of organizing its perception of duration.

Practice of *Frames* can momentarily offset the idea that space and time are fixed instead of relative (and that they therefore control and limit us).

. . . .

Just to There

When you feel overwhelmed
and want to quit,
pick out a landmark just ahead
—a light pole, a house, a tree—
and agree to run
only that far.
Then, as you approach the mark
you set, pick out another one up ahead,
and again decide to run
"just to there."

foot-notes

· ·

Sometimes things seem too much. The sheer blinding mass of change and assorted duties that greet us as a new day dawns can bewilder and threaten to overwhelm us. Focus on what's in front of you and start playing the *Just to There* game.

If you tend to worry, go on a worry fast. Give yourself permission to operate worry-free until noon. Say, "At twelve, I'll worry all I want, but not until then." With practice, you can develop unstop-ability.

recipe for the sole

. . . .

Remember Now

Look back at yourself
from the future.
Remember this present experience
as a fond memory,
a thing of the past.

· ·

Seeing the present as a future memory can make things leap suddenly into focus. It's an easy thing to practice, no matter what you are doing. It's another way to expand your consciousness out from the imprisoning cocoon of clock time, and find yourself in the Momentary Moment all over again.

Time is the Cosmic Joke—it seems to be in such short supply in constant white water yet, properly seen, it's more like rubber. Practice making up new ways to stretch it, and rediscover the truth that you are never the prisoner of time.

. . . .

Effect/Cause

Go unsane. Think flipside.
Switch causes and effects around
as you run, as in:

- I am running because I'm breathing hard.
- The street ends because I'm turning a corner.
- The reason people look at me is that I feel
  self-conscious.
- This time of day is fine for a run because
  that's what I am doing.

foot-notes

· ·

Dreamrunning helps us reshape our perceptions so that we become detached from our "reasons."

Practice unreasonable thinking. Be generous for no reason. Be grateful for no reason. Be happy for no reason.

. . . .

Mainspring

Run like a clock,
imagining a mainspring inside you
slowly uncoiling,
powering you along.
Feel your mechanism hovering between
its push-from-behind and
its pull-from-in-front.

foot-notes

. . . .

Have you ever looked at a clock and seen it for what it is *not?* This mechanism, which often seems to run our lives, can fool us into thinking there actually are intervals called seconds, minutes, and hours, independent of our agreement about it. Although these intervals seem to describe something we are experiencing, the ticking face that measures them, which we invest with such power, is merely the cover of a repeating-machine.

The truth is there is no time, apart from our perception of it. When we keep time we are simply keeping our agreements.

. . . .

Slo-Mo

Get just above knee-high
in a wide expanse of standing water
(lake or low tide at the beach).
Start to run,
feeling the drag of the water.
Lean forward, work your arms,
and delight in running
in true slow motion.

foot-notes

· ·

Whenever possible, run near water—
around a lake or reservoir, along the ocean,
or by a river or stream. Stretch out your
arms toward the water and draw its energy
to you. Study the surface of the water and
feel those feelings within yourself—calm or
rippling or wave-tossed.

Then bring that *Slo-Mo* experience into
the other parts of your day, feeling the
lengthening-out of each fluid moment, so it
all becomes more leisurely, manageable, and
enjoyable.

· ·

Rush Point

As you run, concentrate on the point
ahead of you
where the details of the running surface
blur and all of it spangs out and
rushes toward you.
Think of yourself on a spaceship,
watching the stars
blast by.

Many desktop computers' workstations dis-
play the rush-point on their screen-savers.
Whenever people are not working at their
keyboard, up comes that mesmerizing little
program of the stars endlessly blasting at
them. It's handy for harried people to medi-
tate periodically on that animated cosmic
rush-point during their busy days. It can return them to a sense of their birthright outside of spacetime.

. . . .

Rock-a-bye

Pretend you are running with a limp.
Run harder on one side,
reaching forward with one leg
and braking with the other.
Get a go-stop-go-stop motion going,
rocking forward and back with your upper
body. Think of being rocked in loving
arms. Then see how your mind shuffles the
deck when you switch sides
and run the other gait.

foot-notes

. . . .

Run with your hands over your ears until your attention focuses on the songs of breath-flow and footbeat. Alternate hearing one as the background for the other, then interweave them in a body-instrumental. Merge them into one soothing, dependable concerto.

Learn to listen for changes in the score, the beginnings and endings of movements. Think of what you're hearing as the replay of an ancient recording.

. . . .

Falling

Plummet comfortably
into an unimaginably deep hole,
watching the sides exploding past you
as you relax and fall.
The Cosmic Safety Net
is always there.

foot·notes

· ·

In our mountain ropes course, we came to the rappelling station. I had enjoyed all the other activities, but this one—backing over the edge of a cliff, looking behind me down at the tops of trees hundreds of feet below—had my terror up. The instructor said, "Let go."

I nodded and looked down at my hands, fingers white-knuckled around the rope. Knowing I was strapped safely into the harness, I still resisted that first letting-go. After that, swooping down 20 or 30 feet at a time and bouncing off the rock ledge with my feet was great fun. Human beings have trouble letting go sometimes, but it is the very opposite of effort. You just do it.

. . . .

Running into the Past

Run "back to the future."
Visualize a cassette tape
in which the tape is time,
and the reel of tape already played
is the path on which you are running.
Now behind you
stretches the unknown,
and the road ahead beckons you
toward recent memories.

foot-notes

. . . .

When you think of the past, dwell only on those illuminations, those sacred moments when you were impossibly happy. Revisit those childhood epiphanies, those timeless times when you knew you were a child playing on the lap of the Infinite, and that your place in the Lifeboat was assured.

CHAPTER 6

Connecting with Our True Selves

I celebrate myself, and sing myself,

And what I assume you shall assume,

For every atom belonging to me as good belongs

to you.

I loafe and invite my soul.

Walt Whitman

Dreamrunning trains us to alter our experience of ourselves and our world. The Recipes for the Sole are strategies designed to help us Dream the World (be aware that we are making up reality as we see it); Reframe Experience (shift at will the psychological and emotional meaning of a situation); and Play with Time (have all the time we need for doing what is right to do). *Dreamrunning* changes the way we take in the world and thus lifts us above the petty pace of life. We view things newly, and we are changed by this. The end result is that we become in touch with, or *grok,* our Real Selves.

As we master the practices described here, life becomes transformed. Where formerly we saw scarcity, we now experience abundance. We no longer feel like victims, but artists of our destiny. We gain a special wisdom from which to live, a knowing that comes through us from our True Selves. It is from this place that we *grok*. To unleash this potential, these practices must not become ends in themselves. As effective as they are in de-stressing and focusing our minds amidst all the chaos with which we are presented, they too can become merely a new set of coping skills. They must be placed in service to a higher cause—an overarching purpose based on ideals and values.

VALUES ARE ANCHORS

Dreamrunning allows us to detach from events and make decisions based on right action. What criteria do we use in this decision-making? It is our personal values which we have chosen freely and to which we are committed. Values enable us to renounce the conformity and mediocrity characteristic of the herd, and zig when others zag. Value-driven actions actualize our True Selves. Along with practicing the Recipes, using values as guidelines for actions and decisions is pivotal in achieving harmony with purpose. Living by values gives us a different way to measure what our actions accomplish and frees us from the tyranny of time.

There are two steps to the process of living by values:

1. Identify the values
2. Make the values serve a higher purpose

STEP 1. IDENTIFY THE VALUES

. . . .

Choosing values to live by:

On a sheet of paper, copy those values from the list on the next page that jump out at you. Add your own. Out of that list, choose three. Rank order these to identify your first, second, and third most important values.

truth	freedom	service
sincerity	justice	contribution
trust	hard work	satisfaction
strength	honor	balance
excitement	self control	achievement
learning	love	action
vision	initiative	goodness
creativity	courage	joy
spirituality	friendship	nation
leadership	loyalty	community
perspective	respect	nature
family	fun	work
order	happiness	gratitude
cooperation	beauty	candor
humor	prosperity	_____
persistence	integrity	_____
wisdom	peace	_____
flexibility	clarity	_____

1. _____

2. _____

3. _____

. . . .

Dreamrunning and our values must move us in the direction of an overarching purpose, or they can lose their meaning. The following quotation captures the core experience of *dreamrunning*. When Shaw wrote it, he could have been talking about escaping from *littlethink*.

> This is the true joy in life, the being used for a purpose recognized by yourself as a mighty one; the being thoroughly worn out before you are thrown on the scrap heap; the being a force of Nature instead of a feverish selfish little clod of ailments and grievances complaining that the world will not devote itself to making you happy.
>
> George Bernard Shaw

Shaw's words perfectly express what I have found in *dreamrunning*. He is saying that human beings experience transcendent joy when they find their lives directed by a mighty purpose. All those little concerns of the ego are seen as petty when we are grasped by such a purpose and uplifted to become a *force of Nature*.

Some people may ask, "How can I find my purpose in life?" The question itself suggests that it is a search, a process of figuring something out. Actually, it is the very opposite of that. We are not looking for our Mighty Purpose, It is looking for us. We do not discover our Purpose, It discovers us. A better question might be, "How can I place myself in a position so that my purpose can find me?" One thing is certain: We cannot be "found" if our minds are always full of noise and confusion. If we are asleep in mechanical thinking, or *littlethink*—that solidified mode of reacting to conditions and circumstances where we are always behind, never doing enough—we cannot listen inwardly to hear the Voice that gives us direction. We might be said in that case to be "SILT"—i.e., Stuck In Little Think.

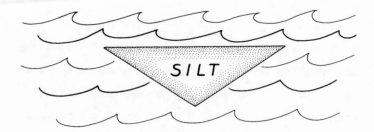

Fill a jar with the muddy water from a turbulent stream and leave it to sit for awhile. When you return, the silt has settled to the bottom, and above it the water is crystal clear. When we are SILT (Stuck in Little Think), our minds are just like that cloudy water drawn from a rushing river. Unable to see through the murkiness of chaotic events speeding at us, we cannot recognize, much less choose, the actions that are right for us. We need to withdraw our energy from all our rushing about in order to stay ahead of the ten-ton truck of change, and allow our minds to settle and clear. Only then can we see what response we need to make to the situation. In order to get to that space of choosing, and to live more and more in it, we must:

Dreamrunner advisory

. . . .

Seek solitude.

Plotinus wrote:

> *The wise man recognizes the idea of the good within him. This he develops by withdrawal into the holy place of his own soul.*

We can achieve the dynamic equilibrium we have lost to constant white water when we establish and maintain what mythologist Joseph Campbell calls a "sacred space"—a time or place we go each day where we quiet ourselves and ask the prime questions: *"What am I really up to? Am I on purpose? What was it that I intended?"* Here we have our relics, those objects and symbols (pictures, books, music, candles) that connect us with our highest selves— that *re-mind* us. Here the world does not intrude; here we can let the urgent stuff go and concentrate on the important.

The world will not give us this time; we have to carve it out for ourselves. It may cost us a half-hour of sleep, getting up earlier in order to enter the day reflectively, but whatever it takes will be worth it. For we will know that we're not, in the words of the flight navigator quoted earlier, "totally lost but making great time." In time and with much practice, *dreamrunning* can become a way to incorporate sacred space into activity. Through Noetic

Practices we can train ourselves away from *littlethink* and into the
space of timeless time. It is likely that success in this endeavor will
not be achieved without commitment of time and effort.

TWO SCENARIOS

. . . .

The two people in the descriptions below have realized they do
not have to think or act like victims of change. They enrich and
reward their lives by taking charge of their own states of consciousness.

Harry is the guy down the street from you. Responding to his
preset internal clock, Harry awakens this morning well before
others in his household. The moment he gains full awareness he
disciplines his mind not to begin dwelling on the events of the
day ahead; instead, he goes through a mental ritual of "entering
his day." In less than a minute, having firmly taken control of his
mind, he rises from bed smiling and relaxed. He goes quietly
downstairs, puts on coffee, and proceeds to a cozy corner of the
den, where he takes up a small, well-worn volume of inspirational
readings from the world's great writers and philosophers. He is
pondering one of these when he hears others stirring.

Harry quickly dresses and takes himself out for his fast-walking constitutional. Already his mind anticipates an important business meeting and is reviewing certain tasks he must accomplish before it starts, so he chooses one of the Playing With Time *dreamrunning* techniques. After three rounds of the block using the Recipe called *Just to There,** he returns home refreshed, his mind calm and his awareness completely in-the-moment. While he drives to work an hour later, our friend practices the Recipe called *River.*† Arriving at his workplace, a relaxed Harry goes calmly to work on his tasks of preparing for the meeting. He has barely begun when the phone on his desk rings. His boss is requesting that he prepare another report for a last-minute agenda item. Harry agrees, hangs up, and goes to work with his full attention on the boss's item. Despite the interruption, he accomplishes all his tasks in time to enjoy a conversation with a colleague before the meeting begins.

In an apartment building across town from Harry's neighborhood, a young single mother named Alison has also been going through a process of "entering her day" before she begins her

*See page 170.
†See page 84.

hectic routine as manager of a sportswear department in a down-
town retail store. Upon rising Alison goes quietly to her extra
bedroom, being careful not to waken her four-year-old daughter.
Donning a set of headphones, she puts on some restful music.
She closes her eyes, sits in yoga posture, and mentally repeats an
ancient Sanskrit poem she has learned.

> *Listen to the Invocation of the Dawn:*
> *Look to this Day. In its brief Course lie all the*
> *Realities, all of the Verities of Life—*
> *The Bliss of Growth, the Glory of Action,*
> *the Splendor of Beauty.*
> *For Yesterday is but a Dream, and*
> *Tomorrow is only a Vision.*
> *But this day well lived makes Yesterday a*
> *Dream of Pleasure,*
> *and every Tomorrow a Vision of Hope!*
> *Look well, then, to This Day,*
> *for it is the Dawning of a New Beginning!*

Following some stretching, Alison takes up a writing book, her
personal journal. Opening to the first page, she rereads her mission statement, a personally crafted assertion which never fails to

inspire and reconnect her with her deepest ideals. She spends a few moments reading back over previous pages, smiling to see how some of the former concerns she wrote about have played out. On a fresh page she enters the current date, writes a few sentences, then puts the book aside. Later, Alison will spend her lunch hour *dreamrunning* in the shopping center greenbelt.

These scenarios suggest the degree of concentration and self-control needed in order to be effective in dealing with the amounts of change that are coming at us. They also illustrate how *dreamrunning* can come to be as routine a habit as brushing one's teeth.

PUTTING WHEELS UNDER IT

As has been said, your ability to *grok* begins with the belief that you already possess the capacity to do it. Your practice of *dreamrunning* will go far to training the *grokking* muscle of your mind. Meanwhile, realize that in each and every day of your life there are situations that provide opportunities to practice changing your mind. You have only to be aware of the inner tip-off. This signal is subtle, but you can train yourself to feel for it. It is the first hint of impatience, irritation, edginess, worry, or upset.

If only that person would stop doing that.
Why did this have to happen now*?*
If I can't finish this by the deadline . . .
Why did I have to get in this *line?*

Whenever you get the "upset signal," stop. Go inside. Let go of trying to control things. Choose a way to "Be Run," to have the situation *do you.* Practice for 20 breaths. In time, you will see that the world is there to practice in. You will recognize that the things you're practicing with are not the point; the practicing is the point.

BEING AT CAUSE

. . . .

Row, row, row your boat
Gently down the stream
Merrily, merrily, merrily, merrily
Life is but a dream.

As kids we sang this song, never dreaming that behind those whimsical words a cosmic truth was whispering. Rowing gently is more than just good advice; it means taking it easy on yourself, seeing life as reverie. If life is indeed only a dream, we need not be afraid, for we cannot really be hurt by it.

To those who see life as a dream, it is a whole new study. By dreaming life, by practicing it consciously as a dream, you discover a wonderful secret; you begin to wake up to what it is all about. Each time you practice *dreamrunning* you set certain laws in motion. Becoming one with Cause, you watch the effects—the gleams, the little Winks that show up. That's when you know you're playing your role. That's when you are "rowing gently."

In his foreword to this book, my friend Ken Blanchard shares an experience where, faced with phenomenal success, he "chose wonderment." In other words, he adopted a childlike fascination, a spirit in which it was obvious to him, regardless of circumstances, that things were unfolding as they should. This, to me, is the way to go through life. It's also what *dreamrunning* is all about.

Appendix

This book's history goes back to 1974, my third year of running. That was when I went to Martha's Vineyard and started the experiments with *dreamrunning* that are included in this book. From the first, when I began recording my running experiences, I thought about compiling them into a book. I was intrigued by the work of Buckminster Fuller, the renowned futurist and design scientist, author of *Critical Path* and *Operating Manual for Spaceship Earth*. I wrote to Fuller, included a copy of the manuscript, and requested that he write an introduction for it. To my surprise and pleasure, he did so. To this date his short but energetic introduction has been an honored keepsake of mine, seen only by a few friends to whom I distributed copies of the earlier manuscript. I include a portion of it here in which Fuller talks about his own experience as a runner.

I started running right from the beginning of my life. It is possible that I ran before I walked. For all of my memory it has seemed much easier to run than to walk. One of my legs is much longer than the other. When walking I feel the difference. When running I do not.

Last year, when 86, my right hip joint deteriorated painfully which stopped my running. I obtained a new painlessly operating plastic hip joint. During convalescence my muscles deteriorated. Arising to walk and walking became unsteady, like a bicycle going too slow. The faster one rides the bicycle, the steadier it becomes. Horses find it easier to trot than to walk. Einstein found 186,000 miles per second to be normal. Any lesser speed, Einstein reasoned—and it later came to be proven—was due to angularly redirecting interferences. Mass is interference locked energy: $e = mc^2$. *The principles at work which Einstein was deducing may be at the heart of what Jim Ballard has been experiencing in his running.*

In 1913, I was on Harvard's cross-country squad. Our coach was Al Schrub, at that time the world's fastest ten-miler. One day he came alongside me as I ran and said, "Why are you running with your hands?" I replied, "I am not doing so." He asked, "Why then are you wasting all that energy to clench tight your fists?" I relaxed my fists. Schrub proceeded to eliminate a dozen ways in which I was wasting energy and I began seemingly to leap effortlessly, almost to fly along. Schrub spurted away from me saying, "Take it easier and go faster."

R. BUCKMINSTER FULLER

Fuller's anecdote bears out what I have found about the needless tendency to store tension on the run. I sometimes see a person running as much up and down or sideways, as forward. All that wiggling and bouncing wastes energy. It's the equivalent of adding distance to the trek. Try while exercising to use the yoga principle of the *edge*—i.e., learn to approach an intuitively perceived threshold of effort, but never cross it into the area of pain. Remind yourself that you are *reframing* running from the way it is popularly conceived. In *dreamrunning,* the running part is the vehicle for practicing the Recipes.

Even though the subject of this book is *dreamrunning,* all of the techniques described can be practiced while walking briskly. Better yet, I recommend you do the *wun-ralking* described in the Introduction.

If you do choose to run, there are a few basics. First of all, if you haven't been exercising, start by running to the end of the block and walking back while practicing one of the recipes. (Lots of people enjoy their first run, and don't realize they are overdoing it; then they sit around sore for days and never go back.) Do the same end-of-the-block routine for three more days. Then increase the distance; go around the block. Build up slowly. The point of this is to maintain your own "come-on" of pleasure and exhilaration. Make it a point to:

Dreamrunner advisory

Always do less than you can.

Here are some running tips:

UPPER BODY

Relax the shoulders, arms, and hands. Let the shoulders down. Don't lock the elbows and don't make fists. Run with hands comfortably semi-open.

HEEL STRIKE

Don't run on the toes or the balls of the feet. The heel should strike firmly first, letting the foot roll forward and off the toe.

DIRECTION

Run in a straight line, without flapping or bobbing up and down. Try to keep the head in a straight line.

Beyond all this, do your dance. Do what feels right.

Typically, a run starts with what I call the clunky feeling. That's when the body is protesting, *Hey, what's this? I don't wanna do this!* It takes a quarter-mile or at least a few minutes for the cells to wake up and stretch and yawn. Then you can feel the machine getting down and into the run. Not until then will you "Be Run." There must be a willingness to go through the barriers, the mental restrictions, and physiological "walls" to reach the other side, where that stuff of life, that you're really after, hangs out. Remember the rule:

Don't hurry. Don't stop.

BEING WRITTEN

It has always felt to me as if this book project has a life and, seemingly, a mind of its own; I have merely served it. The words and ideas came through me, mostly during runs. Again and again I have experienced the joy of "Being Run" which the book talks about. Instead of writing, I have "Been Written."

Another reason I cannot claim this book as my own is the importance of the parts others have played in its becoming. I wish first and foremost to acknowledge Barbara Perman, my friend, editor, and literary guide, whose unerring sense of what reads right and wrong contributed so much to keeping the writing on track. Early on, I learned to trust that often Barbara knew more about what *What's the Rush?* is about than I did. I cannot adequately thank my friend Ken Blanchard, who helps make any enterprise fun and exciting. Not only did Ken contribute the foreword, he has been in on this book from the start, freely sharing his love, his ideas, and his belief in *dreamrunning*. I'm also very grateful to Margret McBride, my literary agent, for her heartfelt vision of what the book could do, and for her loving energy in promoting it. My neighbor Jim Wilson played a big part as a listener and contributor of key ideas, particularly the pyramid model. I owe much to the support of my Scribblers group, Nancy Rose Weeber, Bob Collen, and Nat Reed for their belief in me and this book. I sincerely thank Suzanne Oaks, my editor at Broadway Books, for her commitment to quality and to strengthening and clarifying the ideas in the manuscript. And there are others who, along the way, have shared their energy, their spirit and their kindness, and have given new life to this project and helped it go smoothly—among them Speed Burch, Walt Lamb, Jamie O'Connell and the staff at Paper House, Matt Walker, Jane Gronau, Greg Kaiser, Andree Clearwater, German Perico, Ray Snyder, Ann Campbell, and all my friends at Nancy Jane's restaurant, my "other office." Above all, I bow to Paramahansa Yogananda, my spiritual teacher, and to the other great ones in the line—Babaji, Lahiri Mahasaya, Sri Yukteswar—for their guidance and inspiration in the writing of this book and for imbuing it with their divine love and wisdom.

Dear Reader,

Now that you've read *What's the Rush?,* I need your feedback. How did you like the book? What in particular interested you about it? What use do you plan to make—or have you already made—of the ideas it presents?

I am very interested in receiving responses from readers in the form of comments, suggestions, stories, or new *Recipes for the Sole.* If you choose to put some of your dreamrunning experiences in writing and send them along to me, they may be used in future editions of *What's the Rush?* or a sequel, and you will be credited by name. Please write to:

DREAMRUNNER
P. O. Box 3003
Amherst, MA 01004

Thank you!
James Ballard